Helping the Helpless

One of the streets of lower New York where the Woman's Branch sends its workers, among a population exceeding one million.

Helping the Helpless

In Lower New York

BY

LUCY SEAMAN BAINBRIDGE

Hon. Supt. Woman's Branch, New York City Mission Society

Author of "Round the World Letters"

INTRODUCTION BY

REV. A. F. SCHAUFFLER, D.D.

NEW YORK CHICAGO TORONTO

Fleming H. Revell Company

LONDON AND EDINBURGH

Printed in the United States of America

New York: 158 Fifth Avenue
Chicago: 17 North Wabash Ave.
Toronto: 25 Richmond Street, W.
London: 21 Paternoster Square
Edinburgh: 100 Princes Street

TO

MY SON

WHO HAS EVER BEEN

"MY STRONG STAFF"

INTRODUCTION

BY REV. A. F. SCHAUFFLER, D.D.
President New York City Mission Society

MY long acquaintance with Mrs. Lucy S. Bainbridge has given me abundant opportunity to judge of her work as Superintendent of the Woman's Branch of the New York City Mission Society. For eighteen years she showed great ability and tact in dealing with the difficult problems pertaining to her office. For this she had had abundant preparation, having gone around the world on a kind of missionary tour, inspecting various missionary fields. This experience fitted her peculiarly for undertaking the work in our cosmopolitan city.

With untiring zeal, with marked ability, and with a never-failing courage, she faced and discharged the duties that came to her. Mrs. Bainbridge was peculiarly apt in dealing with individual cases. These characteristics are shown very markedly in the story she has to tell of her dealings with those who are in peculiar danger, morally as well as physically. These stories, true to life, cannot fail to fascinate the sympathetic reader who, on putting the book down, will thank Mrs. Bainbridge for having put pen to paper, to record such thrilling experiences.

In all her work the author has put the *spiritual first*. This has been the policy of the New York City Mission Society from its start. She knows full well that when help extends only to needs material, or even to needs intellectual, the deepest nature of man has not yet been reached. You can clothe a degenerate, and feed him, and house him, and he may still remain a degenerate. Mere "social uplift" does not change man's *character,* and in this world of temptation and sin, our aim should be predominantly that change of character which, if it really takes place, governs the whole life for all time. To this end Mrs. Bainbridge's efforts were always attuned, and the success with which she met was most gratifying and calls for gratitude to God for his Divine assistance.

It is only fair to say, to Mrs. Bainbridge's credit, that if there be any royalty coming to her after publication, she desires to donate it straight to the Treasury of the Woman's Branch of the New York City Mission.

FOREWORD

ROM years of experience in downtown New York I have culled a few incidents of real life, and am putting them in print with several reasons in mind.

I would fain try to help the good work of the Woman's Branch of the New York City Mission Society, of which it was my privilege to be the Superintendent for many years.

To the faithful workers, missionaries and nurses of that Society, who are at all times and in all weathers giving comfort and care, and the love of Christ, among the poor, I would add my word of encouragement and praise.

To those who stand behind these workers, and, by the giving of money, and sympathy, and prayer, keep the work ever moving, belongs a reward that cannot be estimated.

Part of our host have crossed the Flood, but so large-hearted and far-sighted were they, that though we no longer see their faces or hear their voices, their generous support of the work goes on and on. Mrs. Jesup, Mrs. Osborn, Mrs. Dodge, Mrs. Fernald, and others,—all our noble givers,—though called dead, are yet, among many other beneficences, building up the kingdom of Christ on the earth, in downtown New York.

Another reason for recording these simple stories, is that I want my grandchildren, in the years to come, to know and to love the work their grandmother tried to do while she was here.

I have selected these incidents from very many, taking only those that had a good ending. In the work of building up Christian character, whether downtown or elsewhere, there is much need of patience and charity, and there are many disappointments; but why dwell on the dark side—all work for God is really successful. Other real stories, more interesting than these, if told, would bring in a personal element, that would be unfair, perhaps, to those who have lived downtown, in the so-called "slums," and who are to-day, by the blessing of God, in high places of usefulness and dignified position.

In all this work, with its varied demands, not only have we needed the generous support of the members of the Woman's Branch, but the work has demanded Fresh Air money, clothing, the Easter Fund, and the giving and help of such royal girls, as those of the Dobb's Ferry School.

For whatever of good has been accomplished, the praise belongs to all these givers.

L. S. B.

New York City.

CONTENTS

ILLUSTRATIONS

I

"UNDERNEATH ARE THE EVER-LASTING ARMS"

T was a strange sight, that windy afternoon on lower Broadway, to see a tall man of refined, cultured appearance, calling out newspapers in the midst of the small newsboys. Both his accent and his manner were those of an English gentleman.

My errand down town had taken me in the car to the corner where he stood, and I could not pass him by without trying to solve the mystery. "Pardon me," I said, "but you are an English gentleman. May I ask why you are selling papers on this city street?"

"Thank you, madam," he replied, "I am frank to say,—because I am a stranger, I have a sick wife, and have no money."

I told him I was interested in helping just such strangers, and if he would give me his address I would be glad to go to his wife and take a trained nurse.

The next morning, with a City Mission nurse, carrying her bag filled with everything needed for an emergency, I found the high building downtown, the address of which he had given me. The man, himself, was out selling his papers. We stumbled up the dark stairs, flight after flight, littered with broken pieces of plaster from the walls, until at last we reached the top floor, and in the dark hall groped for the door.

In response to our knock an Irishwoman, whose breath was heavy with gin, opened the door and welcomed us. The room into which we were invited had two windows looking out over the street; two beds—or rather one bed, and a sort of "shakedown," where the Irishwoman and her grown son slept; a stove, a table, a few chairs, and the tubs, completed the furnishings.

Opening out of this room was a sort of alcove room, guiltless of windows, but boasting of double doors between it and the front room, the only air and light coming from the front room. Here two lodgers—longshoremen—slept, and as they often worked until late in the night, the doors were left open all the rest of the time.

Next there was a small room, which might have been called a good-sized closet, had it not been for its slanting roof. As it was, it deserved no better name than "pokehole." There was no light, and no air excepting that which came from the front room, through the longshoremen's alcove. Imagine what it meant when the double doors were closed!

In this stifling place, on a bed made up of boards, a straw mattress, and an old comfortable, lay the Englishman's wife. The Irish landlady had been very kind to her, and allowed her the privilege, whenever she was able to get around, of her son's "shakedown" in the front room, with its good air and light.

The story she told us was,—her father in England had died; there was a little money then coming to her; they were young, and wanted to make a place for themselves in life, which did not seem possible to them in England; they came to Manitoba, put their money into a venture there, and seemed to start out well.

One day a high wind swept over the place, a fire broke out, which could not be controlled, and they lost everything they possessed down to their clothing. Then they said to each other:

"If we can only get to New York—that great and prosperous city—we can find work and begin again. We'll surely get along!"

Enough money was gathered together to enable them to take the journey to New York, and to live for a few weeks. The husband, upon reaching the city, tried every avenue possible to get work. He went into office after office, shop after shop, building after building, beginning down on lower Broadway. His shoes became worn, his clothes became shabbier and shabbier, they moved from more comfortable lodgings to cheaper, until at length they reached the miserable place which the Irish landlady could rent to them, at a very low price. When his money had dwindled down to only eight cents, and he had pawned his overcoat, he started out on the street corner to peddle papers.

After three years of married life they were expecting their first little one.

When they were leaving their English home, the Christian mother had given them a Scripture text, which they were always to repeat, and remember as her word to them, —"Underneath are the everlasting arms— the Eternal God is thy refuge." "Never forget it, Mary, whatever country you are in, whatever troubles you may have to face, that God is eternal and His arms are everlasting. Your grandfather was a man of God, and a preacher, and it was his word to me, and now I am passing it on to you. Never stop praying, and always remember that whether you realize it or not, God is your refuge."

And out of the window of the Irish woman's room on the street, high up above the noise and the passers-by, as near to Heaven as she could get, the little English woman, day after day, had stretched out her hands from the window, and said over and over again that text, given her by her mother. Afterward, between grateful tears and smiles she said, "I cried unto the Lord and He heard me,—He sent you in answer to my prayers."

The time for the coming of the little one was at hand, and the prospective mother longed greatly to see her own mother, so they decided to look no longer for work, or to try to make a home for themselves on this side of the Atlantic. Through the British Consulate we secured passage for them on an outgoing steamer for England, and made every preparation for their sailing early the next Saturday morning. But the Thursday night before, the little one came. Then clothing for the mother and baby and necessary comforts for their voyage were provided, by kind friends of our work, and the nurse carrying the baby, and the husband carrying the wife down the stairs, they were put into a cab, and taken to the steamer.

Just before going on board the ship, the grateful man turned to say "good-bye,"—and, as he thanked me again, he said, after much hesitation, "Am I—am I—am I asking too much, if I should ask one more favor—just one more favor?" Visions of his seeking for a big loan of money, the fear that perhaps he had not been as true as we had thought him, came over my mind, and rather coldly I replied that he might tell me of the "one more favor," and I would gladly grant it, if I could.

Again thanking me for all the kindness that had passed through my hands to them, he said "The favor I should like to ask is this—will you please name the baby?" It was a pleasure, indeed, to give to this little English baby, yet American born, the name of my own boy.

Months afterward, I had a letter from the man saying they had had a good voyage, a warm welcome, that the wife and baby were at the mother's home in Sussex, and that he had obtained a fair position.

II

AN ADVERTISEMENT

" WANT to go to New York, Aunt Jennie. I'm tired of this stupid old town. I feel like breaking away and trying for a job where things are moving. If I keep books here in this factory, surely I can get a start at something in New York and work myself up."

It was a pleasant room, with its old-fashioned furniture, dainty curtains, and growing plants, and a canary swinging contentedly in its gilded cage in the bay-window.

A girl sat at the window, gazing intently beyond the little yard into the street with its few passers-by.

With the weekly paper on her lap, and spectacles pushed up on her forehead, an older woman quietly listened, and not until a sigh escaped her lips did the girl turn.

"Viry," and the aunt's voice quivered as she spoke, "You're all I got. You know I can't git along without you. We'll take a trip to New York soon's we can manage it. I do want to git this little mortgage off, and then if anything happens to me you'll have a home clear—a woman can git on putty comf'table if she's got a home—after that we'll go together, and see New York, Viry."

"But that isn't it, Auntie, I can't settle down in this dull old town. Settle down in a prison? Oh, I never can! I go down the same long street—past the same houses—the same store and postoffice—the same old yards, where the same old things are hanging on the lines, except perhaps for a new patch or two. Then at night I come back—same old street—same people. Truly, I am like a prisoner pacing up and down his cell."

"I know how you feel mor'n you think,"

replied the older woman gently, "but it's prison all through life, Viry—if 'tisn't one kind 'tis another. I've found that out. Wa'n't that John Farnum went by just now? Poor fellow! What a sorry time he's had—and now that motherless baby to care for. I'm glad the old aunt has come to help out a spell—old aunts is pretty good to have around sometimes, hey?"

"Oh, you dear Aunt Jennie, I know what you're thinking of," said the girl, as she quickly left her seat at the window, and threw herself down on the floor beside her aunt, putting her head on her lap. And as the twilight gathered, they clung to each other—the old withered hand gently stroking the curly brown head.

"I'll never marry him, Auntie, I just know what you're thinking of—I'll never marry him. He ought never to have believed that story—I suppose I was hasty and spoke too quick, but I was mad, and maybe—well, we're friends again, anyway, and that's what we'll stay now—never, never anything else. He was down at the mill last week and had the baby girl with him—cute little thing. The men talked so loud little Molly put out her arms to come to me, and then cuddled up close, as though she was afraid and wanted a woman to hold her. Don't you think any more about John Farnum, Auntie, that's all past and gone. He's likely to go to Roxton again, and come back engaged to one of those nice girls down there. It's all right. Men can slip away easy when they have trouble. They don't have to stay behind prison bars, do they? Poor Molly didn't stay long, even in her happiness—only a little over a year—and now here's her precious baby—motherless. I'm sorry for her—I'm sorry for myself. Life seems gray and dull—I'm gray—Gray by name and I guess I'm gray by nature—gray inside and gray outside—but there's one thing shines bright, sure, I do love my own dear Aunt Jennie."

Taking the girl's face between her hands, the aunt talked kindly and practically to her about helping other girls of the village, and becoming interested in some of the forms of work and pleasure in the church, of the social, literary and musical life, which really could be found, though in small measure, even in their little town.

"Elviry, have a share in all these things. There's lots of happy doings right here. You're needed—just you. What was it the man said who preached for our minister last Sunday—'Be in harmony with'——"

"With your environment," added the girl, "Be in harmony with your environment, but make it broader every day until it reaches the eternal horizon."

"That's it, I know, but I can't say it. Now, run along, child, to the Song Service. You've got a good voice, Viry. Give out the best you have and the best'll come back to you. I'll have a nice bit of supper ready when you get back, and if you see any lonesome girl ask her to come along with you. There's plenty—for Sunday night is a lonesome time for them that hasn't any home."

Days became weeks, and Elvira Gray's feeble attempts to become a part of the village activities gradually died out; and she trudged along to and from the mill at the other end of the long street, with a mental fog settling down over her heart and her face, until she began to look like her name —gray!

John Farnum had gone away on a long business trip, and his baby, Molly, had been taken to visit the mother's relatives in Roxton.

A paper dropped from the pocket of a Chicago drummer, near her desk, one day at the mill, and as Elvira picked it up she glanced at the advertisements, with the half-thought of finding that some firm in that great city needed a bookkeeper, but her eyes fell on this:

WANTED: A retired business man of New York City, who has been too much engrossed with his work to care for social life, desires correspondence with a young lady under thirty, with a view to matrimony.

"There can't be any harm in it," Elvira said to herself, "and I'll get a little fun. I'm several years under thirty, and he doesn't mention beauty or a fortune—I'll write, just to see what comes of it."

Her letter was soon answered, and followed by others. The "retired business man" explained how he had made his money by denying himself the pleasures most young men indulge in, and now, as the years loomed up before him, he realized the loneliness which would be his. His mother had died, then a sister—he had few relatives and none very near. He was a lonely man, and longed to find just the woman who would be suitable, pleasant and companionable, for his older life.

As the letters grew longer and came more

frequently, and were filled with bright pictures of life in the great Metropolis, the girl's face brightened, and she went daily to and from the mill with the springing step of a few years before.

"Elviry," said the aunt one day, as she stood waiting on the porch for her coming, "you seem so much younger, and the pink has come back into your cheeks a little —been takin' that tonic I urged you to try? Something makes you glad—what is it? But then again you look anxious and worried. I've been watchin' you. Come in—tell me about it." Putting her arm closely about the girl, she continued:

"Viry, I'm too old not to see things—you've got something on your mind—I've been seein' it. I'm the only mother you've got—now, tell me."

With many a halt, with many an excuse, and with much hesitation,. the story of the unknown lover was told. The aunt listened, as the awful fear of all it might mean clutched at her heart. Stifling a groan which arose in her throat, she said:

"Oh, Viry, show me his picture—what is he like—I'm scared for you—how can you tell that it's all right? Oh dear, Oh dear!"

"Now, Auntie, please listen. He has a pretty home—it's what he calls 'a flat'—with nine rooms facing on a small park,—and there's to be a place always for you, always for you. I wrote him about you, and how you had been my mother ever since I was a little baby, and how good you have always been to me, and how I do love you. He says it will give him real happiness to have a room all fitted up for you, and he thinks more of me, he says, for being so true to you."

"But," and the girl's face became a vivid red, as she went on, "he wants me to come on and be there a few weeks to help him to get things fixed up before you come—do you see? He seems a very lonely man, auntie, with few friends."

The unknown bachelor made no mention in his letters about money, but suggested as the apartment was being painted and decorated that his future bride might like to send on any silver, glassware or linen by freight, and he would attend to the unpacking, and so save her the trouble, and have the place seem more homelike when she arrived.

Accordingly, two boxes of treasured keepsakes were packed, crated and shipped; a box of preserves and jellies was also sent, with bill-of-lading to the gentleman in New York.

"Oh, Auntie, I feel really acquainted with Mr. Stemson. I've learned through his letters that he is awfully fond of sweet potatoes, and you know how fine they are, in this part of the country. I'm going to surprise him by sending on a barrel, just before I go, keeping the bill-of-lading, and attending to it myself after I get there.

"Yes, Auntie, I too am sorry he can't come down, and you see him and we be married right here. I've been hoping right along he could—but he says I've no idea how busy a man can be in New York. Even though he is not in active business he has many things to attend to every day. It's likely he has stocks and bonds and banking to look after, and has to go to Wall Street, and all that. But, he will meet me at the train, and if anything should happen to keep him away, or if the train should be over late, I have full directions where I am to go, and I am just to take one of those new cabs called a 'taxi' at the station—so you see how perfectly easy it will be."

"Elviry," interrupted her aunt, "I can't let you go this way. I'm sick with fear—you must let me talk with the pastor, and ask him to find out about this Mr. Stemson—he must know people in New York who can tell whether all this is true, and the man all right. Viry, I can't let you go this way—Oh, I can't! I can't!"

"Nobody is to know, Auntie," said the

girl very decidedly, "until I send the wedding cards. I won't have this village get to talking. They must just think I'm going on a trip to see a friend—that is perfectly true —Mr. Stemson is now my friend. I'll send word as soon as the wedding's over, and if I can—yes, I'll do it—I'll send some wedding cake, and then the people may talk all they want to,—but not one word now. And then soon, very soon, you'll come and we'll be together again. Oh, cheer up, Auntie, cheer up."

Faithfully and patiently the aunt tried to show the girl the danger of trusting a man she knew only through correspondence; urged her to tell their minister, and have him make inquiries, and then, as a last resource, begged to be allowed to accompany her to New York, but all in vain; she found it impossible to change the plans of the headstrong girl.

But when Elvira was starting, with her arm close about the girl, the aunt said,

"Viry, ye won't let me go with ye, but I'll follow ye, and hold ye with my prayers—God's in New York too, and He'll watch over ye."

The Western train came rushing in to the great station three quarters of an hour late. Elvira was swept along with the crowd of passengers, a "red cap" porter seized her bag, and hurried her on to a stand where cabs and taxies were waiting.

"Of course he won't be here now. There's no use looking. I do wonder if I would know him, anyway. A photo is so different, sometimes, and mine of him was taken so long ago."

Such thoughts surged through the girl's mind, as, bewildered and fearful, she allowed herself to be helped into one of the taxies by the "red-cap" porter.

In her new green suit with hat to match, a touch of scarlet at her throat, the color of the wing on her hat, with a still brighter scarlet glowing in her cheeks, the brown-haired girl made a very attractive picture.

On went the taxi, through crowded busy streets, down Fifth Avenue, past shops and shoppers—the girl's heart joyous one moment with the excitement of it all, and then again heavy with fear of the unknown.

"I'll soon write Aunt Jennie how everything is splendid. I'm sure I'm right in coming. I wish I had seen him once, just once, before——"

A feeling of pride braced her as she saw the beautiful shop windows and thought, "I'll be one of these New Yorkers, and soon be in the swim of it all."

Crossing and turning at several streets the taxi stopped at last on East 13th Street.

"This can't be the place—no indeed," and Elvira took out the last letter she had received containing the full address. "Driver, are you sure this is the number I gave you? There must be some mistake!" and her mind flashed back to the past descriptions.

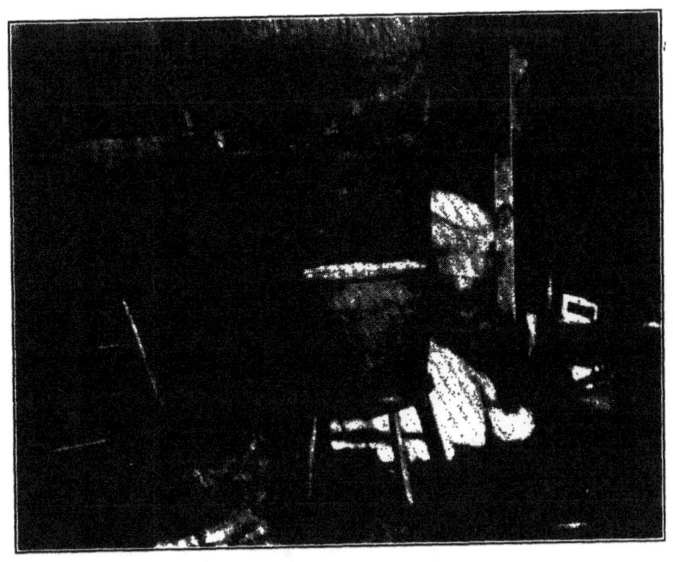

FIVE SONS

were born, in this, the poorest of homes. When the last was a few days old the father complained about such a big family. He went away—has never returned.

A TYPICAL BOY OF THE STREET

"Where is the small park? Where is the 'flat with nine rooms' with 'pleasant outlook on grass and old trees'?"

Helpless and fearful she settled back in the taxi loath to get out.

"Miss, excuse me, but you seem like you didn't know New York. This is the number you give me; and mayhap you don't think about the way a taxi does be eatin' up money—standin' or goin.' It's all to the good for me, but I hate's to see a strange young lady git cheated."

When the taxi with its friendly driver had disappeared and Elvira was left on the pavement alone, bag in hand, her heart sank like lead.

"This is the number. This is the street," she said, as she looked the house over from roof to cellar.

In the basement a Chinaman was busily engaged ironing—too busy to even glance up. At the next floor in one of the windows appeared the sign "Rooms to Let."

The front steps were old and broken and dirty. A man opened the dingy front door, and came out, which gave Elvira a glimpse of the dismal hallway.

"What am I to do—what am I to do!" Elvira asked herself, and then the cheering thought came to her, "Why this is a place, perhaps, where Mr. Stemson has his office; or where he attends to some business, and expects to meet me here and then we can go to the apartment, or to the—church."

This thought brought new courage and the girl mounted the steps, just as a kindly-faced woman opened the door to come out.

"Does Mr. James Stemson have an office here?" she asked, "I mean—is he here now?" and, taking the letters which contained the address from her bag, Elvira looked inquiringly into the face of the woman, who, in turn, was looking the girl over from the top of her pretty green hat to the tip of her new shoes.

"And is it Misther Sthemson ye be wantin' Miss? Yis—he's shure here—he is—took a room three days back—sicond floor—rear." She added to herself, "I'm wonderin' phat the loikes of her is wantin' now of the loikes of him—she looks a dacent little loidy." "If you follow me up I'll show ye his room."

This landlady, whose heart was as big as her capacious body, and whose long experience with men lodgers and their ways in the great city, had made suspicious, was very willing to guide this strange girl up the stairs instead of sending her alone.

With a loud knock at the door with her knuckles, the landlady opened it saying, "It's Misther Sthemson the young loidy be askin' fur."

In one corner of the room by the window, in an old worn easy chair, sat a slouchy, baldheaded man chewing on the stub of a cigar. He was dressed in a cheap plaid suit, and worn russet shoes. A collar lay on the table near him, and his shirt was anything but fresh. He started up from the chair, but dropped back as his eyes were fixed upon the pretty girl, seeming, for the moment, dazed by the attractive picture she made.

"Um-um, Mrs. McCarthy," he said, "Much obliged—um, um—this is my little Daisy come to me from the far away. Come right in, my bird," and putting out his foot drew a chair, as dilapidated as the one in which he sat, toward him without arising. "Come in—come right in—you are—you are a pretty bunch—come in."

The girl stood at the door as though turned to stone. Mrs. McCarthy caught the look of horror on her face and quickly decided it was her duty to stay close by, although the man kept telling her he would not detain her, and now that the young lady he expected had arrived, he had no further need of the landlady's kind services—would she go about her own business?

Mrs. McCarthy smiled broadly and said to

herself, "Biddy McCarthy happens to know her own bisness just at prisent, and that is to sthay close by this gurrl."

Elvira, in a voice shaking with excitement, crossed the threshold of the door and said, "This can't be—oh, it can't be Mr. James Stemson! Oh, say that you are not —who are you? Tell me!"

"Come along in, my Daisy, and let us talk things over—come—don't be scared of me—I'm not so bad, even if I am Jim Stemson." He arose from his lounging position and came toward her. "Come, my Daisy, come in," putting out a long gaunt arm to embrace her. The girl stepped back, just escaping it, and clutched at the arm of the landlady who stood close behind her.

"Come on, my love. We are to go to the man who will marry us to-night. You don't find me as handsome as you expected, do you? Is that it? Well, you look mighty pretty yourself, and dressed to kill—a fine little bird you are."

The man stood eagerly gazing at her, ready to grasp her, but Elvira, holding tightly to the landlady's arm broke forth "I'll never, never marry you. Don't you dare to lay your hands on me—don't you dare! You are not my Mr. Stemson I have had letters from—it's impossible! I must find my Mr. Stemson. You are not he. You are—you are——" "A liar," said the landlady in a loud whisper.

"Go easy—go easy, my bird. You promised to marry me—me—and you're going to stay here with me to-night. You're in New York. I've your promise, and you've come all the way to see me. I didn't bring you. Now take things as you find them and let's get married right away—quick. Come on—be a good sport! I'm a bit down on my luck just now—things have been going a little bad with me. But we can hock that new bag and get enough for a wedding supper, and pay the preacher too." And then, with an oath, he added, "Mrs. McCarthy, will you get out of here? Can't you leave a man alone with his sweetheart?" and he grabbed the door with one hand and took hold of the girl with the other, to pull her into the room. With a scream she threw herself upon the landlady whose great strong arm was about her.

"This is a divil's trap, ye villin," said Mrs. McCarthy in a voice that had in it the ring of power. "I'll be afther exposin' ye, I will—me cousint's husbandt is on the per-lice, and yer name's not Sthemson—mebbe it's one of yer ould names—onyway, this game's all up fer ye—this gurrl sez she won't marry ye, and she shan't."

Cursing Mrs. McCarthy, the girl, and his own bad luck, the man slunk back in his corner muttering that all would have been well if the girl had not trusted to a lying old Irishwoman.

Quickly Mrs. McCarthy slammed to the door, and holding the frightened girl with one arm, led her up the stairs to her own rooms.

"We'll be havin' a cup of hot tay in me own little place. It'll sure warm the cockles of your heart! You need have no fear now—ye can trust Bridget McCarthy, shure!"

The kind-hearted woman did not ask any questions, but after placing the trembling girl in a comfortable seat and slipping off her hat, talked on in cheering tones, telling how she lived in the two rooms and more than paid her rent by taking care of the house; of how she had a woman two days in the week to do the heavy cleaning; of how her husband Patrick, worked on a boat on The Sound, and was gone three days and home three days; of how the extra day of the week he sometimes had to be in Bridgeport and sometimes in New York.

Somehow, the welcome, the hot tea and the feeling of safety, in the little room of the strong woman, warmed the girl's heart into confiding her story to Mrs. McCarthy and asking her advice.

"You poor darlint, now, I'm glad I was to home this day. I had been thinkin' of goin' up to me cousint's for a bit of a visit, but I was here and could save ye, Praise the Lord, from that ould villin. This night me man is here, but he's lavin' airly the 'morrow. The best I can do fer ye I'll do. There's not an empty bed in all this place, and onyway I wouldn't trust you away from me this night, for ye're safe with Biddy McCarthy—I'll be contrivin' somethin'."

With a soap box at her feet, and an old quilt on a wooden chair to soften it, Elvira was put into the small room of the McCarthy home, which was really a closet, where pails and tubs and ice-chest were kept.

All through that long night the girl sat listening to the heavy breathing of Patrick McCarthy in the next room, thinking, thinking, praying, wondering what she was to do.

In the small hours of the night Mrs. McCarthy on tiptoe opened the door a crack and whispered, "How are ye gettin' on, me dear? Me man makes a foine noise—I hope it doesn't throuble ye. Sometoimes it do be loike the band on Saint Pathrick's Day. Don't be scart—will ye? Ow, that ould rat of a man! That ould villin! I'm indade glad I was home this day."

"Phwat's that, Biddy," said a voice from under the bed covers, in the next room, "You heard a rat? Wait 'til the mornin' thin catch it; set yer trap."

The next day Mr. McCarthy was off on his three-day job, and Elvira was cuddled into his side of the bed, where she was told to "lay shtill and be aisy in her moind."

Sleep was impossible, but as she rested and prayed, the question "What am I to do?" kept saying itself over and over again. Though the door was kept locked, she started in fear at every sound outside. But Mrs. McCarthy, doing her cleaning of halls and stairs, kept one ear toward the room of her lodger.

"I can't go home; I can't stay here," was the constant cry in the girl's heart. "What will I do? Oh, supposing Mrs. McCarthy had not been here! God has helped me—Oh, He will—but how?"

The check for her trunk was still in her possession, and a few dollars in her purse. With many misgivings Elvira found her way to the head office of the railroad, on Broadway, and inquired whether or not they would take her few dollars, keep her trunk as security, and let her have a through ticket to Millville. If so she would surely return the money, the very day she reached her home.

The clerk informed her that this arrangement was impossible; that the railroad must have cash for the ticket. At that moment an elderly man came forward, from the rear of the office, and asked her a few questions gently and kindly. "We cannot grant you this favor, I'm sorry to say, but take my card to a lady—a friend of mine—who will perhaps be able to advise you what to do."

The lady to whom this railroad official sent Elvira was the writer of this little story.

It was not difficult for an experienced and sympathetic woman to draw from the girl the real facts in the case, although at first there was an effort on her part to invent a little tale and avoid the real truth. Having the whole story, the work of helping the girl could be taken hold of with loving zeal.

A missionary — a practical Christian worker in the crowded tenements — was ready for service. She started right out with Elvira to the house on East 13th Street, where Mrs. McCarthy was anxiously awaiting the return of her "darlint."

The three then went together to Mr. Stemson's room, where he was still lounging, filling the smoke from his pipe with curses on his bad luck. They informed him, in no uncertain tones, that his supposed victim was in the hands of friends. He threatened and swore and called Elvira the vilest names he could think of. He would let her village friends know her real character. He would tell them——

The strain of the journey, the fear and excitement and lack of sleep had made the girl really too ill to travel. Fortunate was it that the son of the writer was a physician, ready to give any help. Rest, comfort and care were also given the poor, frightened girl.

The missionary found that Mr. Stemson's "place of business" was a low Bowery saloon, where he washed the glasses and cleaned up the floor when he was not selling liquor over the counter.

The man had had a fair education in early life and had married a dressmaker; while she lived and supported him he kept up a semblance of manhood, but after her death, through liquor, petty gambling and laziness, he easily slid down the hill of respectability, into the gutter of low saloon life.

After a visit to the freight offices, two of the boxes which Elvira had sent to this man were finally located in the basement of the saloon, and had not been opened. With the help of a policeman and the charge, "goods held under false pretences," they were allowed to take possession of them, and they were afterward shipped back to Millville.

The third box, filled with preserves and jellies, Stemson had sold to a pawnbroker, whose children were enjoying one of the jars when Elvira and the missionary arrived at the shop. The barrel of sweet-potatoes was taken from the freight office and given away.

Money was loaned, a through ticket with sleeper secured at reduced rates, and a grateful, happy and wiser girl was taken to the station, and stayed with until the train started.

Much wiser was Elvira than when she arrived in the great Metropolis. Some of the lessons she had learned were, that though New York has many wicked and unscrupulous people, and while there are many traps laid for unwary feet, yet there is a host of men and women, full of goodness and generosity and Christian love, ready to lend a hand to the foolish and unfortunate.

"Good-bye—may God bless you," said the girl with a happy face. "Good-bye. I never, never can hope to repay you for your goodness to me."

Everyone in Millville said Elvira Gray was greatly changed by her trip to New York—she seemed so sweet, now, and kind and happy; yet they thought it very strange that she never talked about her journey, or told them about the good times she had had in the great city.

A few months later there was a wedding

in the village church in Millville, and Elvira Gray became Mrs. John Farnum. When they were planning their honeymoon, John said, "Elvy, where shall we go for our pleasure trip?"

"Anywhere—anywhere, John," was the answer, "anywhere, except to New York. I never want to see that city again."

III

ALL ROADS LEAD TO NEW YORK

A WOMAN, and little girl of about twelve years of age, came into my room at the Bible House, some years ago, bringing a note from a railroad official asking me to kindly advise the woman, who had begged for a reduced ticket for the child.

The woman and girl were so nearly alike that it was almost amusing, the one was such a miniature copy of the other,—the same dark eyes, the same shaped nose and mouth, and even their voices had the same tone and accent.

"This is your little girl?" I said to the woman. "No," she replied, shifting her eyes from one to another, "no, she is no relation to me; I picked her up on a train as I was coming from the West, she was travelling alone, and I felt sorry for her,—I went to the railroad company to get a ticket for her, so I could take her back, to where she says she came from; I feel very sorry for her." During this explanation the child's eyes became wet and her face flushed, as she clenched her little hands together, but said nothing. "Do you think you could have forgotten? Are you sure that this is not your little child?" "Oh, yes," replied the woman, bracing up to the lie she had told, "I never saw her before until on the train nearly to New York; if I had the money I would buy her a ticket myself, but I haven't enough."

The child responded to my kindness as I put my arm around her, laying her head for a moment against my shoulder, as she sobbed. "You see," said the woman, "she is a dear little thing and I want to take her back to where, she says, her home is."

A FUTURE CITIZEN

Taking little sister with him to school. Later he will join a Fresh Air party for a fortnight in the country.

All my questioning brought out only the statement that the child was an utter stranger, made each time in a more and more positive tone.

Then, at last I thanked the woman for her loving interest in the little waif, and told her that as she was no relation, and had no claim upon her, I would help, and the child would be placed in good care until her family could be found, and then I would see that she was sent to them.

The woman's face flushed, her eyes roved from one to another, she started to speak, and after a moment's silence said, "If I had the money I'd stay near by to see what you do with her, at least a few days. I got very interested in her seeing her on a train alone."

The Home for Homeless Girls welcomed Dora, and a place near by was secured for the woman. Two days later, as I had expected, the woman came to herself, broke down, and with tears and sobs said, "O, I lied, I have lied; I have committed the unpardonable sin; I have disowned my own child; I'm going away where she can't see me. I am a sinner; I have lied—lied; I know you will be good to her, and by and by I'll send money and have her come to me."

Everything was done at the Home to make Dora happy, but at night she would sob herself to sleep, saying over and over, "Oh, my mother told a lie, my mother said I was not her little girl—that awful lie." The child grew pale and sick, under the strain, notwithstanding the loving home life around her. After a few weeks we received a letter from the mother, from Cleveland, saying she had a good position working out by the day, and had a little home of two rooms, and would like to have the child sent on to her—she would return us the money, if we would advance it. Every effort was made to find out more about the mother. From all reports she was industrious and an earnest churchgoer, devoted to a small mission, where she was very active. Having friends in Cleveland, upon whom to rely in case of need, we decided that it was best to let the little girl go to her mother, and share the mother's life. We fitted her out with comfortable clothing, and away she went under the care of a travelling friend, as happy as a child can be. Her last word as she left us was, "my mother does love me I know; she is sorry for that awful lie."

Before leaving me I sewed into her pocket a small stamped envelope addressed to myself, and said to her: "Dora, your mother does love you, and I hope you are going to have very good times with her, but if any kind of trouble comes, and you need a friend, send this little envelope back to me, and I will understand and try to help you. Two months had passed when I received in the mail my envelope, and inside was a little note from a neighbor, a woman who lodged in the same house with Dora and her mother.

"For God's sake, lady, get this child away from here; she is getting killed." My friend in Cleveland found the home, and the child and her mother; everything seemed all right. It was put to the mother that Dora was looking a little pale, and wouldn't the mother like her to take a trip to New York, with my friend, for her health's sake. The mother's consent was gained provided I would promise to have her taught French.

After reaching the station the mother suddenly changed her mind, and just as my friend got the child inside the gates and was entering the car, the mother, with a scream, tried to follow, and get on the train without a ticket, but was pushed back just as it started.

Little Dora reached New York as pitiful a little girl as anyone would want to see; she was thin, haggard and sad. Her story was this:—Her mother was a missionary worker believing the end of the world was close at hand. She wanted her child to follow in her footsteps, and be ready. She took her to meetings every night, and brought her home to her rooms, and then soaked the girl's feet in cold water above the knees, so as to extract the evil from her nature. The mother fed her with ashes, for the purification of her soul, and when the child refused she would sharpen the great butcher knife she had, and draw the back of the knife across her neck, telling her that God had told her to punish her, and that she would put the sharp edge on if she said a word.

Besides being thin and wretched, Dora came back with a hard cough, which we found immediately was whooping-cough. The Home for Homeless Girls, of course, could not take her in. There was no institution or suitable place in the great city for her under the circumstances, but, fortunately, in my own home there was no one who would be endangered, so that Dora came to me, and for over a year, was my own devoted, happy child. Measles followed the whooping-cough, after which she went to public school.

In the meantime, by correspondence, we began a search for her relatives, and discovered that there was an uncle by marriage, in the far West, who had been alienated from Dora's mother for years. At last there was a welcome for the child with her own people.

A little girl about her size, the daughter of one of the ladies interested in our work, passed on to the Heavenly Home, and the clothing she no longer needed just fitted our waif. Well clothed, with her pretty travelling suit and coat, Dora, who was now a bright, cheery girl, was taken by the Children's Aid Society, to the West.

There, in the home of her uncle, she learned to play the little organ, and was a very happy and useful girl.

Years after, Dora married, and she and her husband went still farther west into Oklahoma, took up a claim of unoccupied land, and in a little rough log cabin lived until they owned the land. In this log cabin she gathered her nearest neighbors for a Sunday service, and with the aid of her little organ made it very attractive. The young man, to whom Dora gave her heart, did not prove as true and steadfast as she could hope, and finally deserted her; but Dora's Christian character has stood every test. She is now filling a good position in the far Southwest, yet ever longing to come once more to New York.

IV

MY SANCTUM

HEN the City Mission offices were moved from the old Bible House to the new and commodious building of the United Charities, furnished by the generosity of Mr. John S. Kennedy, a very cosy, comfortable room was fitted up for the Superintendent of the Woman's Branch. Beside the regular furnishings of desk, chair, etc., there was a comfortable rocker, willow lounge, and ornaments on the mantelpiece, which gave it a very homelike atmosphere.

Into this sanctum came, from day to day, very many and very varied people, with all kinds of trouble.

A young man, a stranger in New York, had touched the work of our society, and, in his longing for companionship other than that of the cheap boarding house where he lived, came in at his noon hour, to ask me how he could get acquainted with some nice girls. His home circle, in the small town where he had lived, had been very dear to him, with cousins and aunts and friendly young people, but New York was a wilderness, and he felt utterly forlorn.

At another time a gentleman called who wished the door quite closed during his interview, and then confidentially told me of the death of his very lovely and educated wife and the utter loneliness which had followed. He could not find another helpmate in his own country parish, and needed a woman as nearly like his wife as possible, who could help him with church work, and read over his sermons, and make practical suggestions. Would I think over his need, and introduce him to some attractive lady missionary of the Woman's Branch?

One visitor was a young man from a far distant mission station who had gone out alone, was home on his furlough, but did not want to return without a helpmate. He found all the girls he used to know and like, married and, as he said, "the younger girls don't seem to care for much beside tango, and we don't have that kind out where I live." He needed a little advice about a certain young lady he had heard I knew very well. Suffice to say he returned to his mission field with a very suitable and charming wife.

Another caller was a woman so decorated with chains and beads and rings and bracelets, that it was difficult to know whether she was a Hottentot or an American. She had a business venture which would make any one investing largely in it very rich indeed—the returns would be sure and large and speedy. I was given the opportunity of thus becoming a millionaire on the condition that I give her the names of rich women who knew me, and a letter to each endorsing the scheme, and gaining for her entrance to their homes for private interviews. It is needless to say that neither to her nor to any other person, for any cause whatever, did I give names or letters of this kind.

One morning a sad-faced young woman in black came in, whose story ran like this: Her husband was dying with tuberculosis; his people were paying for him to have the care he needed in a sanitarium, but it was an incurable case. She had been living with her father, but now he had died, and she must find work to support herself and her little two-year-old girl. Her husband's people were not able to help her, and she did not know which way to turn. The blue eyes filled with tears as she told of how little strength she had for the battle of labor outside of home, and how she had prayed for courage. "Oh, I must find work," she said, "and I must find work where I can keep my little girl with me.

Don't tell me that that will be impossible."

A caller in the main office outside was demanding my attention, and telling her to make herself comfortable in the rocking chair, until we could see what could be done, what plan could be devised to help her to help herself, I went out to meet a young man, strong, alert, earnest, who said, "You perhaps don't remember me, Mrs. Bainbridge, but I know you, and I have come because I think you can help me. You know my two little girls have no mother; poor Mary died a year ago. I have tried to keep things together by hiring different kinds of women to help, but it's no go. The other day I went home from my job and found things just worse than crooked. Now, I can't stop my work to stay home, and I've got to find somebody who will be good to my children. I can hire the scrubbing and washing; I can't afford two or three servants, but I have a good little home on Long Island, partly paid for. I want somebody that'll keep my home and be good to my kiddies."

"Will you take a very nice little woman, with her two-year-old child? She cannot do the heavy washing and scrubbing, but she can cook, and keep your home, and I am sure would be very kind to your little ones."

He stopped a moment to think, then gave his leg a vigorous slap, saying, "By George, that's the thing exactly. Where can I find her?"

"She is here," I replied, "waiting for you."

A little later I looked out of the window, and watched the two walking off together.

Perhaps it was two or three years afterward that the same young man came into the office and greeted me most cordially.

"I had to come," he said, "to thank you for giving to my children and to my home one of the best little women in all this big world. She's my wife now, and here's a photograph I brought to show you."

It was a family group.

"Here," he said, "are my two children and me; this is her child and here she is; and this little boy in her lap—fine little fellow, isn't he?—is ours."

Into this Sanctum came nurse or missionary to talk over and get light on the many problems of drink and poverty and sickness encountered from day to day.

How much to help, what agencies to use, how best to make those helped learn thereby to help themselves,—all these and many other questions had to be talked over. Ever bearing in mind, in all our work, that it was not a ministry to bodies alone, with that help given, we endeavored to reach minds and souls, and to build up Christian character.

V.

A TENEMENT DAISY

ITS of plaster were broken off from the dirty walls, the wood-work was dingy and the floor even worse, in a room where a woman, bending over a sewing-machine, sat close to an unwashed window which looked out upon a court filled with clothes-lines, overflowing garbage barrels and other refuse. Her dress was faded and ragged and her hair in disorder, yet, notwithstanding this, real beauty of form and features could readily be seen, and it was not difficult to believe that in her younger days the woman had served as an artists's model.

On the floor in the centre of the room sat a man and his two-year-old boy playing together with straws and tiny sticks. In a dark corner a little girl was doubled up in an old, worn-out, broken-down rocking-chair, minus a rocker, trying to shield her inflamed eyes from even the dim light. The noise of the rattling old sewing-machine drowned the sound of the knock, and as the missionary caller stepped into the room the man gave a start, looked up curiously for an instant, then went on playing with the child.

The sewing-machine was slowed up and, after a greeting from her caller, the woman said in a low voice, pointing to her husband and touching her head in a significant way: "He's bad to-day—was in the sun yesterday awhile. Things goes hard with me. My cough ain't no better,—keeps me awake and makes him mad. Mary don't seem to never get over the measles. He says she's goin' to get blind."

An opportunity to go with a special Fresh Air party, where the girl would be well looked after and have all the milk and

A LITTLE CURLY-HEAD

Under the tangled hair and the dirt there can be found by a loving hand, beauty and sweetness, and a soul.

eggs she wanted, with fresh air and green grass and farm life, was pictured by the visitor. "Apples, big trees, tiny chicks," muttered the girl in the dark corner, repeating some of the words she heard,—"Oh, I'd love it!"

The difficulty of proper clothes and shoes was to be met, and the visitor would come in two days and take little Mary to the train.

At the appointed hour the missionary knocked again at the tenement door. No rumble of sewing-machine this time, but the mother, in a gruff voice called out: "Who's there? Come in!" The man was asleep in an inner room,—or it might better be called a closet,—the little girl was again huddled up in the same old chair, stifling her sobs.

"I've made up my mind not to let her go. It's all nonsense, anyway. I thought you'd try to make me, for the child won't stop her snivelling, so I just put them new things where 'twould put an end to it." In a tub of dirty water were to be seen the new gingham dress, and the new stockings and shoes which the missionary had left for the girl the day before.

An empty bottle and a breath laden with gin explained the change of plan. But after some moments of plain speaking, in a most forcible manner, with the accompaniment of pitiful sobbing from the dark corner, the mother's heart got the better of her drunken brain and it was decided that "next time" Mary might go.

Experience is a good teacher, and when that next Fresh Air party was selected, the missionary was up with the sun-rising, and carrying the clothes with her, washed and dressed little Mary herself. Dark glasses over the still weak eyes were a real comfort, and little Mary was at the station, by eight o'clock, as happy a child as any in the party.

There was a loving welcome at the end

of the journey, in an ideal old farmhouse, where

> "The trees fold their green arms about it,
> Great trees a century old,
> And the winds go chanting through them,
> While the sunbeams drop their gold."

Here the little girl found more than care and good food. Her mind and soul expanded to the beauty surrounding her.

A lily, pure and beautiful, will grow in darkest mud. The most fragrant blossoms of early spring are found hidden under the fallen leaves and mossy carpet of the woods, and many a human flower when taken from the wretched conditions of tenement life will grow and mature into beauty and fragrance of life.

Before the time for Mary's return, the farmer wrote:

"Dear Lady:

"Will you please try to get our little Mary's people to allow her to stay longer. She is getting stronger and her eyes are much improved. We all love her. Even the dog and the chickens will miss her. We must keep her."

Meantime, things were happening in the tenement house which Mary called home. The baby brother suddenly sickened and died. The father, who could not bear the sunlight and had been obliged to take his outings by night, was stricken with grief. He was frank in saying, "My boy was wuth while, but girls ain't no good. Let the child stay. She ain't no use anyway."

The sunstroke, which the man said he had had when working on a high building, kept him at home during the daytime, but at night he had been in the habit of going out for the air and to pick up an odd job. He evidently picked up something beside the odd jobs, and this something he tucked away in a high cupboard of the dark closet, —bright things, bracelets, watches and chains. No one ever saw these in the daytime.

One winter's night, the year before Mary's trip to the country, when her father was handling a glittering piece, Mary woke up and asked him to let her see it. The child never asked again, for the reply was that if she ever told anybody or asked any questions he would take the hatchet,—which he grabbed and brandished over her,—and cut her head open and chop out her tongue. His fiery eyes and ugly voice made the threat one never to be forgotten by the child.

After the death of the little boy, while Mary was still at the farm, in an unwise moment the father confided to his janitor that he had found in an alley-way a good watch, and gave it to him in return for some special privileges. Not long after this a prying policeman visited the tenement and asked some pointed questions of Mary's mother about the watch and the man's business. The father, who was hiding not only from the sunlight but from visitors like the blue-coated policemen, took the first chance to slip out the back way and disappear.

Later a scrawly, unsigned postal was received by Mary's mother. Soon after she turned over the key of her room to the agent of the building, and went away,—where, no one knew. The other tenants were all too busy and too tired in their own struggle to live to give more than a passing thought to the disappearance of their neighbors. The mission nurse in her work found the rooms empty. It was just the time for Mary's return. Was the child on the train? What could be done to keep Mary from returning to the desolate place. A telegram to the farmer who had taken the girl and asked to keep her, reached the farm just as Mary was bidding the dear people good-bye. It was a very happy girl who unpacked her little bundle and stayed on.

Nothing was really known of the child's mother after that sudden departure. The woman's cough and her drinking had been growing from bad to worse, so it is probable that in some other city than New York she has filled a pauper's grave.

Is it too great a stretch of the imagination to think that this man, who disliked the sunshine and took his outings in the darkness of the night, has been spending his time in some old greystone building with iron bars to shut out the light and to shut him into the dark?

Mary gradually became a loving member of the farm life, and fitted in as though it had always been her home. At first she talked little, but often chattered in a low voice to the chickens and the flowers, which were her companions. The little girl would nestle down among the daisies, silently watching the fleecy clouds sail by, or sit for hours weaving daisy chains for her neck and hair.

"Where is my little girl?" called out the farmer to the child almost hidden in the grass, her head crowned with daisies. "Won't our little Queen of the Daisies come now for some dinner?" And so smilingly did she run to take his hand that her name after that was "Daisy." Later, at school and church and in the village, no one knew her by any other name. The whole of her own old name slipped out of mind. Miss Daisy grew up as a daughter,—a capable, lovely young woman.

To-day, in a position of trust and large influence, as a well-educated Christian woman, she has been able to return to her foster-parents in their times of trouble real comfort and help. In prosperity or adversity, and now in older years, it is Daisy they love and lean upon.

VI

A COMPANION

MRS. BROWN was convalescent. The skill of the surgeon had resulted favorably. There had been trained nurses and physicians and now she was getting better, but was still very nervous and not at all strong.

"What I want," she said to her doctor one day, "is not to see a nurse's uniform—it reminds me too forcibly of ether, the instruments, and the pain. I believe I could get well quicker if I had a bright, pretty young woman to talk to me and read to me and thus make me forget my illness."

A relative of Mrs. Brown had a friend who knew of a girl who, she thought, might fit this place. All she knew about her was that she was ladylike and refined, and had been very good to her mother who had been sick for some time before her death. The young woman wanted a position, for her father had quickly laid aside his mourning and married a young girl who wanted the whole house to herself.

Soon after this, the motherless girl was installed in the comfortable home of Mrs. Brown. She gave the tonic and the medicine, read aloud, arranged the flowers, and sometimes sang little old-fashioned airs, when the invalid was nervous. Indeed, Laura was like a daughter instead of an employee in the home.

After many months of this work, even in the delightful surroundings of this elegant home, Laura grew restless and chafed at the monotony of her life. "There is no future—no outlook in this kind of a position, and it is now that I must obtain training for larger things," she thought.

Instead of confiding in Mrs. Brown, who

was more than an employer, Laura carefully studied the advertisements in the papers and answered one which she felt was the very gateway to fortune. A New York man offered training and salary to good-looking girls of cultured manners and some knowledge of music.

Such a vision of a splendid future arose before the girl that she answered this advertisement and was accepted before Mrs. Brown had been told. "I wish you could have trusted me, Laura," she said. "I feel like a mother to you. When I am strong again I will gladly help you to some training in music. I appreciate your humdrum life here in this small town, and being with a complaining old lady. You have been good to me. I hope you will not go, Laura—and surely do not go alone to meet an utter stranger."

But the girl felt that she had given her word, and anyway, it was too fine an opportunity to miss, and the indefinite promise of Mrs. Brown reminded her of the old saying, "A bird in the hand is worth two in the bush."

The gentleman at the head of the Musical Bureau had very kindly agreed to meet her at the station, and the girl was instructed to tie a handkerchief around her right arm, so that she might be easily identified in the crowd. So Laura went on to New York from Ohio, and her correspondent met her as he promised. He was a fine-looking, well-groomed, well-dressed, person and talked pleasantly with her as they met. He called a cab for her, suggested that she hand him her check, and said he would gladly relieve her of all trouble regarding her baggage.

As they rode along he told her that he would have her voice tried in a day or two, but in the meantime she must rest from her long journey, and he would take her to a good boarding house, where she would be very comfortable. On arrival at the place designated, they found that the lady of the house was out, but he showed Laura to a room which she could occupy until the landlady's return. As he had important business which would keep him until evening, he would go and she could make herself known to the family, and later he would explain the kind of position, the training needed for it, and the salary she might expect.

As the gentleman was about to leave, however, he suggested that it might be wise for her to allow him to put any money she had with her into the safe. Servants could not be trusted always, especially in New York, as she had doubtless heard, and there were many pickpockets and sneak thieves in the great city. Laura thanked him as he took her roll of bills to put in a secure place, and bowed himself most politely out of the room.

In the elegant room with its long mirror, lace curtains and fine furniture, Laura sat down in an easy chair to rest. Feeling very much alone, and as she afterward said, with a strange fear clutching at her heart, she opened her traveling bag, took from it her tiny pocket testament, and turned for comfort to some of the sweet old verses about God's care for those who trust in Him.

A cleaning woman was scrubbing the marble floor in the hall, and because of her great loneliness and longing for human companionship, Laura opened the door a little and left it so. The woman on her knees with her cloth and her pail of suds stopped now and then to look in at the girl as she sat there reading the little book. Finally, the woman with hesitation beckoned the girl to come nearer the door, and said to her in a whisper:

"Do you know what kind of a house you're in? I'm a decent woman—I have to earn my livin'—I comes here to clean twice every week. They thinks I don't know, but this is one of the devil's own houses. I'm sure you won't tell on me—but if you're what I thinks you are you'll git out while you can git out. The missus has gone to the the-a-tre, the door is well locked, but I'll open it prentendin' I'm cleanin' the marble beside it, and you can git out. You'd better be lively for some of 'em 'll be back before long."

Laura had just fifty cents in money in her pocket and it was nearly night. Was it true, she thought, if she waited to get her money from the safe that she could not get away that night? What did the man mean? There were sounds at that moment on the floor above which made Laura decide quickly, and taking her bag she was soon on the street, walking, but she knew not whither—down—down—wondering—fearing—praying—until nightfall.

On a corner she saw a policeman whose face looked honest and kind, and she asked him to direct her to a lodging-house for women, a cheap but respectable place. He not only gave her the address, but pointed the way so clearly she could not miss it.

The next morning, when she went to pay for her night's lodging, she told part of her story to the matron. This woman was in touch with our work in lower New York and it was not long before the girl was safely in our hands.

Upon my desk that morning lay a letter received the day before from a lady who was not a stranger, whose beautiful home with its many surrounding acres of ground overlooked the Hudson. This lady had written telling her needs:

> "You know my Jamie; the attendant who has been with my crippled lad has had to go away. I do not suppose you can help me find just the right one—it is hardly in your line—but I do want to find a bright, sweet young lady—one we can take right into our home and make one of us, who will read to Jamie and amuse him. But I wish—and I do feel this is too much to expect—I wish I could find someone with enough of the gift of music to sing to him when those distressing spells of his come on. The dear little boy does suffer so at times, as you know."

This letter had not been answered. Laura was sent there, and proved to more than meet their needs. Later they wrote thanking us for sending them "such a bonnie song-bird," and adding that Jamie was already devoted to her.

It might have been a year after that, as I sat one morning in my little inner room, that someone slipped up behind my chair and then a pair of arms were placed close about my neck, a face touched my cheek, and a sweet girlish voice said, "Oh, I must thank you this way for saving me!"

Not long after this it was reported that someone else beside little Jamie was devoted to the "bonnie song-bird" and that it was Jamie's big, good Uncle James.

VII

A LITTLE PROPERTY

N the basement of a tall house, on the lower east side of New York, lived a cobbler who hammered away at old shoes which were brought to him to mend by people who were too poor to buy new ones. He was obliged to work very close to the window, and even there the light was dim, as the room was below the sidewalk. At the rear, where the window was only three feet from the next high building, his wife, Sophie, did their scanty cooking, and kept the little home, as tidy as she could by the dim light of an old, smoky, oil lamp.

It was a damp, dreary place, full of the odor of old leather, this home into which little baby Sophie came. Not long after the birth of the child, though the nurse of the City Mission gave her the best of care, the mother slipped away from the dismal basement and left Peter, the cobbler, and their baby girl most forlorn.

On the third floor of this high building lived a German woman, who was considered the grand lady of the house. She had two windows toward the street, where the sun shone in a part of the day through the old lace curtains. When the children of all the homes above this grand lady, away up to the roof, came trooping down the stairs, they were always eager to stop, and get a peek through the crack of the door, to catch a glimpse of old Mrs. Schmidt's elegance. There was a stuffed sofa which had once been red and purple and green and yellow, but they never noticed that one leg was gone and that it was propped up with a board. There were two chairs covered with the same flowered stuff, except for the patches, one of which, if you called upon Mrs. Schmidt she would carefully keep you from sitting on, for one leg was past repair. There was a gay lambrequin, with fringe, a big vase on the mantelpiece, a picture of Bismarck in a gilt frame, and other things which had once been whole, but were now so broken and chipped as to have lost all suggestion of any former use or beauty.

Mrs. Schmidt didn't have to work very much, for at frequent intervals there came to her registered letters from Germany. The other tenants of the house,—the O'Raffertys, the Timonses, and those of different nationalities, — stood in awe of Mrs. Schmidt, for she had little to say and held her head rather high. And so, when she went down the stairs, dressed in her good black dress and long gold chain, with a white feather in her hat, they felt that this grand lady gave tone to the whole building.

When little Sophie was born, Mrs. Schmidt's big heart, in her capacious body,

LITTLE BURDEN BEARERS

At different centers on Friday, afternoons, we hold what is called "Children's Hour," with stories and songs. Here, all the little ones are welcomed.

grew very warm and it led her to look in on the Polish family in the basement. After the little mother's body was carried away she went down into the midst of the bits of leather, and said kindly to the stricken husband and father: "I 'ave a goot place up de stairs, an' no childer. If you like ter lent me de baby avhile I vill take care uv 'er fer you, den you can turn yerself already."

A dozen other families in the house would have done the same, for the poor are ever ready to help the poor, but Mrs. Schmidt had the sunshine, and did not have to go out to work and leave her door locked, letting the child stay alone. The missionary nurse was ready to visit and care for the baby just the same as though it had staid with its father, so little Sophie became a part of Mrs. Schmidt's elegant home, and took possession of Mrs. Schmidt's big heart.

A few years passed by, and Sophie was

old enough to join the primary Sunday School class, which the missionary nurse conducted most interestingly every Sunday morning. Mrs. Schmidt had no use for religion,—she had gotten above the Bible and its superstitions. Invitations to attend the German service were always refused, and she was quite unwilling that Sophie should have anything to do with a church. But the little girl's eagerness to go, and her love for the nurse, at last overcame the old woman's reluctance, and a compromise was made. If Mrs. Schmidt could go with Sophie and sit on one side, and understand what was going on there, she would let Sophie go to Sunday School. After that, the two were to be seen in the primary class Sunday after Sunday. Later on, the child coaxed her foster-mother into the preaching service, and the gospel seed found good ground, took root, grew and blossomed, and Mrs. Schmidt became an earnest member of the German Church.

When Sophie was about six years old, Mrs. Schmidt was taken ill. The attacks of pain, from which she had suffered, increased and the old woman began to realize that the time would come, and perhaps suddenly, when the little girl she loved would be left without her care.

"I vant mine leetle girl to 'ave mine leetle property," she said, "an' we must not let her to de basement go. She is mine own leetle one." A young German lawyer was found, who made her will at a reasonable price. Not many weeks after, sudden death came, as she had feared, and the same lawyer helped us settle up the estate, which amounted, when all debts were paid, to about one hundred dollars.

In the meantime, old Peter, the cobbler,—feeling that his child was well cared for,—had drifted away to another city, and to some other employment. The one hundred dollars was put into a savings bank in the name of Sophie, but we were made trustees or guardians.

The summer before Mrs. Schmidt died, as she was not then well, we gained her consent for Sophie to go with a Fresh Air party to a farmer's home in the western part of the State. Upon her return to the city, after a stay of only a few weeks, the girl had such red cheeks and bright eyes, and told such glowing stories of the beautiful woods, and the farmer's home, the old woman was fairly jealous and declared that the next time Sophie was asked she would go, too.

"I want this same little girl next summer," wrote the farmer. "There's a standing invitation for Sophie to come and stay as long as her folks will let her——"

This welcome came to mind very forcibly, as we closed the tenement rooms, sold the old furniture, and asked ourselves the question, what should be done with Sophie?

For a few weeks we took the lonely girl

into our own home. But what was the best plan for a long future? A half-orphan asylum would give good care and training, but better than any institution would be a Christian home where, as a foster-child, she could have personal love.

Letters were sent and answered, and the farmer and his wife made ready a pretty room, with toys and books, and then welcomed the coming of this little girl as their own.

A year later, I was staying for a time at a hotel within driving distance of the farm, and decided to pay them a visit. Letters had been exchanged between the foster-father and ourselves as to Sophie's future, and he knew all that we did of her family, and the "little property" in the savings bank.

As our carriage drove up, along the lane leading to the farmhouse, the farmer was returning from the fields with a load of hay. Through the vines, at the side of the porch, we could see a group of little girls dressed in white playing and laughing and setting out a table for refreshments. In the centre was Sophie, in a pretty white dress, her hair adorned with blue ribbons. "Mother said I might play this is my birthday," she said, after greeting us, "and these girls are in the same Sunday School class with me, so you see this is my birthday party, and I'm so glad you got here! But you haven't come—you haven't come to take me away?"

The farmer left his load, and with a hearty smile and hand-grasp made us welcome. After a little waiting, he said: "It wouldn't be strange, not knowing me, if you should think I wanted to keep the girl, because of that hundred dollars rollin' up interest. You see her name ain't Sophie Polinsky any more, she is Ruth Rollins, and I'm business man enough to know that if anything happened she'll never get a cent of it,—leastways without a lot of trouble.

We want to keep her, and send her to school, and bring her up, and we've given her our name; and now just to prove that I mean business, and to save that money for her, when maybe she'll need it by-and-by, if you choose to trust me to put it in the savings bank here in this nearby town, where the girl can get it by-and-by, when she needs it, I'll put in just the same amount of money for her myself." Suiting the action to the word, he pulled from the depths of his trousers' pocket,—under the overalls he wore,—a hundred dollars, and laid it down with a slap. "There it is, and I'll add on the interest to a penny when I know exactly what it is."

In that home, Sophie,—now daughter Ruth,—has been loved and trained and prepared for life. As a young lady in the social circle of the village she makes no stir. She is not beautiful of face or figure. She cannot boast of great learning, but Ruth can bake bread, and cake good enough for a county fair. She can mend, and make, and best of all she has the art of being happy, and making everyone happy in the home where she lives.

The children all love her and old people enjoy visiting with her. She makes a good teacher of the primary class in the Sunday School. She has no special talent, yet every one agrees she is a comfortable girl to live with.

"A commonplace life we say, and we sigh;
But why do we sigh as we say?
For a commonplace sun in a commonplace sky,
Makes up a commonplace day."

VIII

FRAULEIN

HE love part of a story is usually at the end. After many difficulties and much misunderstanding the hero tells his lady fair what she knew all the time perfectly well, the wedding follows and the curtain falls.

Not so with this simple, but true little tale. It must begin with the fact that Fritz loved the blue-eyed Christina, and had not only told her so, but had also stated that fact to his own family, to Christina's old grandfather and to his frau—Christina's step-grandmother.

"This marriage, Fritz," said his mother, "will be impossible. I am sorry, but we have other plans for you. Christina is a sweet girl and will make some fine young man a good haus-frau, but not our Fritz—our only son. The girl we have selected for you is of good family, beautiful, and with a fat dowry. From what we are told she will not only keep your house well—she can knit and sew and cook—but she can also sing and play. We have it all arranged with her parents, who quite agree with us that it will be a proper marriage. She is an only daughter and you are our only son. There will be much money coming to you from both families. You will be a rich man by and by."

German authority is not often questioned, and Fritz was a loyal and obedient son.

"Mother," he said, "I shall not marry Christina while you are unwilling to receive her. She and I can wait. I shall not leave her and she loves me. Liebe mutter, no other girl in all the world do I want—only my own little sweetheart. I cannot marry anyone else. The girl with the fat dowry will not want a man whose heart is elsewhere. I shall stay with you, but I shall never marry anyone but my own little Christina."

In a cottage home beyond the town, several miles from the large mansion where dwelt the parents of Fritz, Christina lived with her old grandfather. They had been told frankly about the decision which had been made by the parents of her lover. The girl and the old grandfather were much to each other, and she opened her heart to him.

"I cannot stay here. I must go away. I cannot see my Fritz married to another girl. They will surely force him into it. He is so good and loves his father and mother so much, he will have to please them. You know, grandfather, how we Germans are—how we feel when an only son does not have a house and home and family. Oh, I cannot stay. Will you let me go with the Sister who is going back to her work in America? She says she will train me—she has a school for girls who want to do good, and will take good care of me. I don't want to leave you, my dear good grandfather, but—oh, I cannot stay!" And with sobs choking her voice she threw her arms around the old man's neck—"I cannot stay and see Fritz married to that girl. By and by, after I am trained, I will come back and take care of you, and help poor sick people. I won't mind then."

A few days after this the Sister from America, dressed in a peculiar garb, called at Christina's home and added her persuasion to the entreaties of the girl. Promises were given for a careful training in attractive work, and at last the grandfather yielded and with trembling hands gave over to the German woman from America the sum of money she required for the passage, training and care of the girl.

After much preparation the last day came and it seemed as though the old man's heart would break to part from Christina. "God is my trust in this awful darkness," he said. "He will never leave nor forsake my little one. He rules the wind and the waves and He will keep you safe on this great voyage. His promises will hold like an anchor even in far off America."

Then came the last good-bye, and the saintly old man with wet cheeks, with one arm clinging around the girl and the other raised to Heaven, with solemn voice prayed, "May the Lord watch over you. May the Lord guard and guide you, my precious one. May the good God bring you back to my heart and home before I go hence."

The steamboat express for Hamburg must always keep schedule time. It could stop only for a moment at the junction for a delayed train and then must rush on. So a long thin trail of smoke was all that could be seen of this express as a German-American lady hurried from the train on the branch road. "How annoying," she said. "I've lost that train, and so I have lost my steamer—oh, why—why?" At Hamburg other plans had to be made, and in a few days this traveler had joined the motley throng on the deck of another ship bound for New York.

Peculiar people, and customs which would look strange on the city street, excite little notice in the crowd of passengers on board an ocean liner. But the German-American lady's attention was directed, almost before the ship left the pier, to two women dressed in a peculiar garb. The contrast between these two women held the lady's attention—one of them was young, pretty, and timid appearing; the other was middle aged, plain, and with a decidedly aggressive manner. The dress was black, made with a full skirt and sleeves; the waist was pleated. The bonnet was made of white linen and tied underneath the chin with strings of white linen, while attached to the plain front-piece which surrounded the face was a full crown, hanging loosely and forming a sort of broad collar which extended well out on the shoulders.

In their promenade up and down the deck the younger woman began to tire, and the older one tucked her into a steamer chair, bidding her rest, but to be sure to have nothing whatever to say to anyone. Was it "chance" that placed the German-American lady's steamer chair next to the one occupied by Christina, or was it in answer to prayer?

Back and forth paced the older woman until a group playing cards attracted her, first into watching and then into joining in the game. After a bit drinks were ordered, she was urged to share, and seemed nothing loath to join in this also.

Little Fraulein was very obedient and sat quietly in her chair, but the sad, lonely-looking girl presented a very pathetic picture. So thought the occupant of the chair next to her and she realized that the mist and spray sent up by old Ocean could not be responsible for all the moisture that filled the blue eyes and trickled down the white cheek.

Unable to use or even understand a word of English, Fraulein could all the better obey the command, "Make no words with anyone!" The German-American lady ventured to express a bit of sympathy in the tongue of the Fatherland, but all her efforts were quietly repulsed. After a while, however, the girl's heart warmed under the kindly words and more kindly tone, and when the older woman was out of sight, little by little Fraulein told a part of her story, and as the days went by the two travelers side by side became very good friends.

"The Sister is really very good," said the girl, "and is kind to the sick and the poor. There are so many poor Germans in New York City that she has a house for them and a little hospital and a training school, too. She has been to Germany before and told about her work and people have given her money; and grandfather paid her to give me the training. I did not want to stay at home now—there is a good reason. I will go back, by and by, when my Fritz is married and settled down. You see, the Sister came to our house and she knew I was unhappy, she offered to take me, to train me in her school. My parents are dead. Dear old grandfather did not want me to come—if he had not been willing I would not have come. He cried and said it would kill him if his little girl went away to far off America—by and by I will go back—after I get the training."

"Where is this school, or house, where you are going with the Sister?" asked the lady.

"It is on an avenue—I do not know just where—of course, New York City is a very big place—the Sister did not tell me just where."

In God's great plan this German-American lady was a trained nurse in the City Mission service, working among the sick and the poor of the crowded East Side in New York City. Her large experience made her feel troubled about this simple-hearted girl. Was she being deceived?

Fraulein, however, was confident that everything was all right and that the Sister was really very good. Had not her friends trusted her and had not her dear old grandfather trusted her? She surely must be all right.

But this did not satisfy her new found friend. So she wrote out full directions in both English and German, making it very clear how this girl could find her, if at any time she might need a friend in the great city. After a little urging Fraulein took the slip of paper and promised to say nothing about it to the Sister.

In the confusion of landing and with customs examination the German-American lady found it impossible to follow the strange pair to learn where the Sister lived; then came the needs of the work crowding in upon her, until the meeting with the sad little German girl became merely an incident of the voyage and passed from her mind for the moment.

It was not so very long after this, however, that a little German note, enclosed in the very envelope she herself had directed, found its way into the hands of the German-American lady, and it told her that Fraulein did need a friend, and needed one right away, and gave instructions where she could be found.

Very promptly the lady responded by hunting up the place. She found the house most forbidding, with its closely locked doors and drawn shades, while there was not a sound within. The door was tried again and again but in vain, so she stood waiting for a moment, then in the distance she saw the Sister coming, followed by Fraulein, each carrying a basket of food.

In a loud angry voice the Sister asked the caller what she wanted and then ordered her away and told her to mind her own business. Fraulein was commanded not to speak to her. The door was opened, and shut quickly with a bang in the vistor's face, and locked from the inside.

A sobbing appeal was heard to please let her talk to the good kind lady just one moment. This was followed by the slamming of another door on the inside—and then silence reigned.

The next day the German-American lady, who was not so easily frightened, called at the house again. The Sister had gone out evidently thinking the reception of the day before would have the desired results. Tremblingly little Fraulein unlocked the great door and let her in; and clinging to her the girl told her story.

There was no training—there was no hospital—she was kept scrubbing and washing, and then she had to go out with the Sister begging for food. When she was not out with the Sister she was locked in. She had been told she must not write to her grandfather at present—that the letter written by the Sister was quite sufficient.

At night all sorts of men and boys called and she had to make special soup for them, greasy and thick. Some of the men stayed all night and talked to her—English was hard to understand—but it sounded bad, and they looked at her in a way she did not like—she was afraid and hungry and homesick. The Sister was very cross and said she had not been paid enough money, that she must learn to eat the soup, or earn money in some way, and that she must stop crying. "Oh," Fraulein added, "if only I could get away—can you not take me? I shall die here—I feel afraid all the time. Oh, if only my grandfather knew!"

This visit was cut short by the return of the Sister, who was very angry at this second intrusion of the strange woman.

The next visit was made with an officer in citizen's clothes. The Sister was told that the girl was of age and able to decide for herself, that she had come to America for training which had been paid for and which she was not receiving, that the German-American lady was ready to assist the girl to secure what she desired, and that she had come to take Fraulein away at her own request.

This brought forth a perfect tornado of vile, indecent words and curses, which was quieted only when the officer's badge was disclosed and the woman warned that such language would lead to her arrest.

Then she launched forth upon a perfect sea of abuse, charging Fraulein with ingratitude and wickedness; telling her she was no good whatever to her; that if she went away with that strange woman she would surely be taken into a bad life; that the home people should be told by the next mail how their little Fraulein had gone to the devil; that when the old grandfather knew it it would kill him; and that he was going to know the worst, and, too, that not one penny of the money would be given back; that the girl should not receive one cent, and that her trunk must stay right there.

It had been arranged to have an expressman ready outside, and at last, with another flash of the officer's glittering badge and a view of the determined look on his face, the trunk was brought forth. But the Sister could not let it go without venting her anger still further, by giving the trunk such a vicious kick with her heavy shoes that the lock was broken, declaring there must be something in that trunk that belonged to her, for the girl was surely a thief, and would be sent to jail. "And then," she added, "your friends in Germany will realize how bad you are!"

The officer helped the trembling girl out of the house, and as she went down the steps she turned to say "Good-bye," whereat the Sister, in a more violent attack of rage, hurled the broom after her, calling out, "Thief! Thief!!" and quickly picking up a stick that lay by, she placed it across the broom thus making the sign of the cross, and standing beside it, she spat after the departing trio.

Suitable clothing, a warm welcome and loving care were given to the little Fraulein, who gratefully responded to every kindness. To the City Mission leader and to others who learned to love her, she was like a sweet friend. But to the City Mission nurse the girl clung most lovingly, fearing to allow her out of her sight. "My dear little rescue mother—my little rescue mother," she would say.

A letter giving information about the Society and its Christian work was sent to the home people in Germany, but not before the Sister had sent her story about the "ungrateful and wicked girl" having gone into a life of sin, and how she feared they would never see their pretty Fraulein again.

Soon after the rescue of Fraulein, and while she was under my care, it so happened that the son of the superintendent, with a patient, two Christian gentlemen, were to sail for Germany to spend several months. They talked with Fraulein, learned about her people, and took letters from her to them. On their arrival in the German city, they settled down near her home for a short time to strengthen their knowledge of the German language, and made a few friends of the same Christian character as themselves.

It was Sunday afternoon, when they went to find the home of Fraulein in the suburbs of the city. Word had been sent to the grandfather, and in the parlor he was leading a religious meeting and prayer service for his little girl so far away. Her letter and the letter from the strange American gentleman were so different from those sent by the Sister that it was impossible for the friends to understand what it all meant. "Can our Fraulein be a thief?"

one had asked the other. "Has she truly gone wrong? Why did she leave the training school—why? What is this Mission Society? Who was the strange lady on the steamer?" "Wait," said the grandfather, "wait—wait and pray and trust, and let us believe our little girl's story until we know more."

At the close of the service the American gentlemen made themselves known, and presented letters, pictures and other proofs of their statements. The aged grandfather listened intently to every word, standing all the while as though in prayer, his face as white as the silver hair which crowned it. At the close he turned quickly and threw his arms about the neck of the younger man and kissed him on both cheeks. Little Fraulein was vindicated! And the rejoicing in that household can only be likened to the joy of Heaven.

While Christina was in America the rich girl, selected for Fritz, took her affairs into her own hands and decided she would not wait for a lover who had told her he loved another girl, and so she carried her dowry into a family glad to receive her; and a grand wedding followed.

The parents of Fritz began to be anxious; they did not enjoy having a bachelor son. Where was the Fraulein? Would she soon return? What were these reports about her? Who were these two American gentlemen staying in the city? After hearing the reports of these two gentlemen, their hearts went out to the poor, brave little girl, and the mother said: "Perhaps, after all, Fritz should marry Christina and not wait any longer for us to find some other girl for him!"

So kindly letters were sent and little Fraulein, who was always busy in New York helping in many ways in the work which her "Rescue Mother" was doing among the poor, began to sing as she worked, and the sad look in her face turned into quiet smiles.

Although the Sister had given that trunk

a hard blow, the lock could be mended, and when Christina's busy fingers had finished the pretty garments she made for herself, she filled it, and was ready to sail away to the homeland.

This time she did not travel in the queer garb of a make-believe Sister, but in a very becoming dark blue traveling suit and hat. And it was not a sad, pale-faced Fraulein, but a Fraulein with pink cheeks and bright eyes that waved "Good-bye" from the deck of the steamer to her American friends on the shore.

And when that same steamer docked on the other side of the great ocean, the first one to meet and greet the home-comer was Fritz, loving and loyal Fritz,—and he had with him his parents' blessing.

There was great rejoicing when they reached the home of Fraulein's old grandfather. He had been prostrated with grief and anxiety, but grew strong with the joy of seeing his loved one again. And at the wedding which soon followed, he laid his hands on their bowed heads and blessed them, while a glory shone in his face—the glory into which he soon after entered forever.

The German-American lady made another visit to her Fatherland, and one summer day, without writing, she took the journey and rang the door bell at Mr. and Mrs. Fritz's home.

"Who is it—a stranger?" questioned Mrs. Fritz, coming forward with her baby boy in her arms; but when she caught sight of her visitor, she gave a little scream of delight, and cried, "Meine Erlösende Mutter! My Rescue Mother!"

Some years later I visited Germany and this nurse was with me. Together we found the new and comfortable home of Mr. and Mrs. Fritz. Business was neglected that day, and two sturdy boys helped to welcome "mother's friends" from far-off America.

IX

BONNIE MARY

OM McKEEVER felt sure that bad luck was his portion. At any rate he had had nothing but bad luck ever since he crossed the ocean with his pretty English wife and began life in New York.

First he had been taken sick; then the blue-eyed Mary came, and a year afterward the baby's mother died, leaving her to the father's care.

His bad luck continued, and the worst luck of all—so he said—was when he decided to marry the widow with six children for the sake of a home and care for the dear little bonnie Mary. His idea had been that his earnings would be well spent by the widow and that she would love his little girl for her own sake, and it would be easier for him to care for her in that way, than alone in a room in a tenement house. But rheumatism, which had been part of Tom McKeever's bad luck, struck his heart one day, and Bonnie Mary was left an orphan in the great city.

The step-mother had a hard struggle to pay the rent of the three small rooms, and as for food and clothes, there was not enough to go around for her own six. After these were but half fed, and lacked shoes, and were provided with only much-patched clothing, there was really nothing left for little Mary.

One of our workers among the poor and needy found little Mary ragged and hungry, uncared for and unloved. In spite of rags and dirt she was a beautiful child, with large blue eyes, dimpled cheek, and her fair hair in little ringlets all over her head. She was most affectionate, too, responding to every kindness.

The widow was most happy to pass the child over to anyone who could care for her. A plan was carried out for boarding her on a farm in the country, for a small sum, until we should know what to do with her permanently. The out-of-door life, with good milk and plenty of it, made little Mary grow still more beautiful.

One day a lady, dressed in the height of fashion, drove up to the Charities Building and found her way into my inner sanctum. She had heard that sometimes in our work we found pretty little children, who were alone and might prove very promising, if they had good care. She wanted to adopt a pretty, fair-haired child and bring her up as her own daughter. She told of her town house and her mansion at a leading watering place, of how she and her husband had talked it over and decided that their home would be happier and brighter with a little daughter growing up into womanhood in it.

Little Mary was sent for and seemed to satisfy every desire of the lady's heart. Gingham dresses and aprons and heavy shoes were left behind, and the finest muslins, the daintiest embroidery and beautiful ribbons were provided by the new foster mother.

Thus attired the child was indeed in keeping with her elegant home. Clinging to the hand of her new mother, little Mary was helped into the carriage by the footman as though she had always lived in luxury.

Several months later the same carriage drew up before our building, the same elegant lady with her husband following came again into my inner sanctum, the child with them, tenderly clinging to the man she called "dear papa." While the lady talked with me the little girl sat in the man's lap stroking his cheek and loving him with all her childish heart.

"I have come," said the elegant madam, with cold dignity, "to return this child. She is a very dear little thing and seems to love us, and we love her—indeed my husband has become altogether too fond of her to be wise—but I cannot keep her. You should have shown me the scar on her neck. I shall want any daughter of mine to have a brilliant social life, of course, and this scar would be noticed when she wore evening gowns. I tried to see whether pearls would hide it, but they do not, so I have decided on the whole I had best return her." And without further ado she swept from the room and the foster father with tears in his eyes gave Bonnie Mary a loving hug and kiss and disappeared in the wake of his elegant wife.

Back to the farm little Mary was sent. The fine muslin and dainty embroidery were exchanged for the gingham and the heavy shoes.

God's ways are not man's ways. The Scotch father and English mother had been praying people, and though they had gone, their little one was not forgotten by Him who cares for even the sparrows. There was waiting for the coming of little Mary a Christian home with a welcome that endures.

Hundreds of miles from New York, in a quiet town, lived a family of cultured, Christian people, not over-wealthy, but with means enough for refinement and comfort—but there was no child. The wife had tried in vain to find the kind of little girl they wanted to adopt. At last a distant relative of limited income decided to give up to her one of her own little ones. Every arrangement was made to welcome the child—a room with dainty bed and playthings were ready, but when the would-be foster mother went to get the child to take her to her heart and home, the relative found she could not keep her promise, and was absolutely unwilling to part with her child. Back home the childless woman went, so disappointed that she resolved never to try again.

By chance (but is there any chance with God's children) she wrote to a friend in New York that she had just decided that a childless home was her portion, and never again would she think of finding a little girl whom she could love. That letter reached the friend at just the right time. Promptly a reply was sent. "Don't be discouraged if the child you wanted was denied you. Will you not consider the adoption of a little Scotch-English girl whom we will send right out to you?" The answer was "Send her."

To-day in that home, in that college town, there is a young lady daughter—beautiful, refined, well-educated—a perfect treasure to every one in the home; and yet if she should wear a low-necked evening gown, someone would notice a fine line of a scar, over an inch long, on her neck. Her name is Bonnie Mary.

X

"KETCHED UP"

"T seems, somehow, I never get ketched up. Rent day comes awful quick, John has had slack times with his work, the children has been sick, and so everything just gets ahead of me.

"You see, when I was married, I had a little saved up for a rainy day, even after I had bought some pretty good things,—blankets and sheets and towels and all that. We begun to live pretty nice, and I made up my mind that no matter what come, I was going to keep a little tidy home, and have a shiny place, but I can't. I gets so tired and discouraged,—seems no use to try some times. If only I could once get ketched up, maybe I'd have some courage to go on."

As the missionary listened, she saw a tub half full of soiled clothes which had been put to soak; the cupboard was in disorder; the table was covered with the crumbs and dishes of the breakfast. Little Elsie, wrapped in a ragged quilt, was asleep in the middle of the miserable bed.

It certainly looked hopeless, even to the missionary, who was accustomed to seeing poverty and disorder.

Here was an American woman, who knew what a tidy home meant, and, while the man's wages were small, they were not reduced by drink. What could be done?

Talking it over together that evening, we resolved to make an effort to give the little woman a chance to get "ketched up for once."

Soon after this there was to be an all-day excursion for the Sunday School, and tickets were promised to the mother and children, who were urged to go.

"Thank you," said the man, "no ticket for me. I'll take this chance to go out and see a man in the country who owes me some money. Let the children go, and I'll meet 'em when the boat lands, and help 'em get home."

By a little strategy the hiding place of the door key was made known, and when the mother and children and the father had all gone for the day, we took possession of the tenement home. A boarding-school girl, with a generous heart, had sent us from her allowance a gift of money to be used for something or somebody special, and this was now our "special." A poor widow on the next street, who we knew was fighting hard to be ready for rent day, was sent for; around the corner was a young man out of work, who was glad of a job.

What a day that was, of battle with dirt and disorder! And it ended only when the shadows told us that the family would soon return. The clothes had been washed and hung out to dry; the floor had been scrubbed; the stove was shining like new; the shelves of the cupboard were clean, covered with papers, and bright with a row of canned groceries. A new blanket and sheets and pillow-cases made the bed a very different place. At the windows were hung cheap scrim curtains, and the table was covered with white oilcloth and decorated with a small growing plant.

A neighbor, as we worked, peeked in to see what was going on, and ran to the grocer's wife at the corner to tell her, so both came to gaze and admire. They were shortly followed by the wife of the butcher, who went away talking to herself,—a house-cleaning song without music.

The brightened tea-kettle was singing cheerily as the father helped the tired wife and stumbling children up the stairs. Just outside, at a turn of the dark hall, we were hiding.

As the key was turned in the lock, and the door pushed open, the man started back, exclaiming, "Oh, my God! we have been turned out! Somebody has moved in while we were gone!" But little Elsie said, "No, father, it is our place; see, there's grandfather's picture!"

Upon the table, near the plate of cold meat and the bread, we had left an open Bible, kept open by a knife and fork laid across the page, at these words, "Bless the Lord, Oh my soul, and forget not all his benefits."

Thus we gave Mrs. A. a chance to get "ketched up."

Did it pay? Yes!

XI

AGED PILGRIMS

HILDREN, big and little, chattering in a dozen different tongues, swarm up and down tenement stairs, overflowing onto the sidewalk and into the gutters; but tucked away in the dark basement, and up under the roof in the attic, are the old people. They must live where rents are cheapest. The time is past when they can earn enough for shelter and reasonable food, and to-morrow holds out no promise for better things. They are in the land where it is always afternoon, and they cling to the tiny room, which, though poor and shabby, is home, waiting for the call to that home where they shall hunger no more.

In that memorable winter of the panic, when so many of the wheels of industry had stopped turning, charity had to devise work for starving people of all ages and kinds.

In our searchings that winter we found an old lady who had known better days, up under the very eaves of the building, her only window a small skylight. Work had stopped and hunger had resulted in weakness, until she was not able to go up and down the long stairs. There, in her little home, she was found and fed, and later placed in a home for aged women.

For many years an old German couple had lived in a basement on B——— Street. The dilapidated blinds on the windows had to be kept closed, for the sidewalk was higher than the room, and mischievous boys had found their fun in making the cracks of the window glass a little larger by pushing apple and banana peelings through the openings. This front room was parlor and kitchen, dining room and bedroom, and the rear room was the shop, where the old tinker tried to mend umbrellas and all sorts of tin ware. But the push-cart peddlers and the five-cent emporiums had so vied with each other in reducing the price of kitchen ware that the housewife in that locality preferred to buy shining new tins, rather than pay for mending the old ones.

By odd jobs, as holding a horse on a busy street, or carrying a heavy market basket, a nickel now and then was added to the small revenue from the shop, and the old couple were enabled, for a good while, to earn their rent, and bread, minus butter. The little wife had ever done her share by scrubbing, washing and knitting, until that merciless fiend, rheumatism, gripped her hands and knees. Forty years ago their three children, two boys and a girl, were tucked away to their last sleep in the Lutheran Cemetery. In their old age the parents were alone, except for each other.

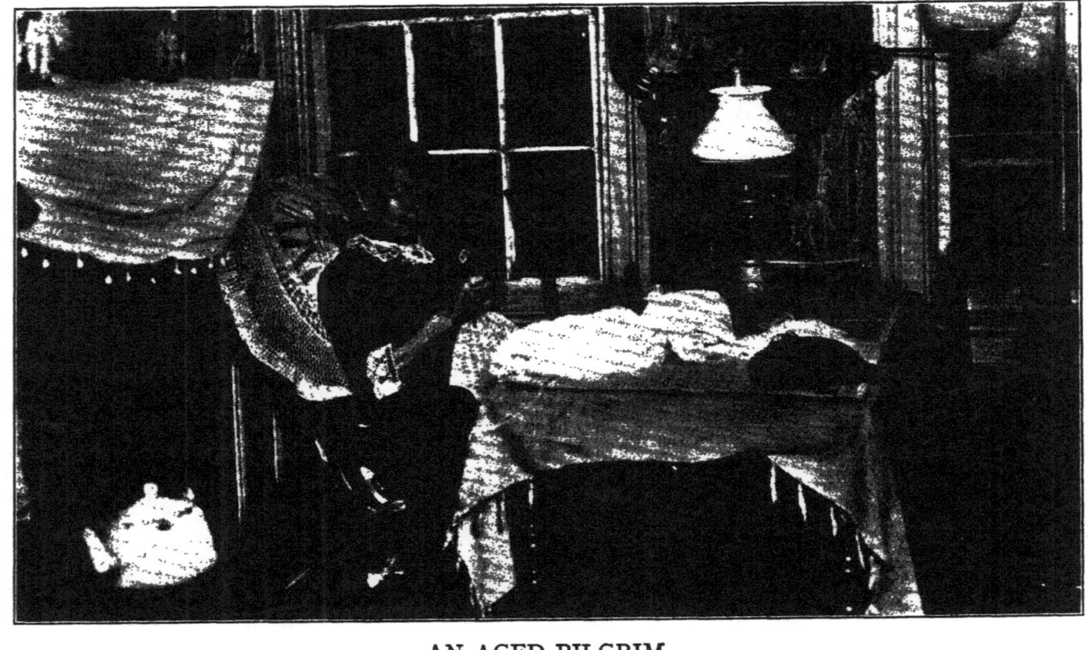

AN AGED PILGRIM

Sunny and sweet, nearly blind and very lame. She crotchets baby jackets all day long, but needs the help given by a generous friend, to live.

They dreaded separation in the almshouse more than death. Since the young lives were gone there was no incentive to learn English, and so beyond a few stray words they used or understood only the language of the Fatherland.

One glad day, before this battle for bread had turned finally against them, word came from across the ocean that a relative, the last of their kin, had died and willed them a small sum for their old age. After legal knots were untied and red tape unwound, and a German lawyer well paid, the balance of the legacy was placed in their hands. "A staff for our old age when we grow feeble and lame, thank God, Ein feste Burg ist unser Gott," they said, as they counted over the dollars. In a great, strong building on the Bowery this staff would be safe, for just as long as they could work they would not lean upon it.

A neat, leather-covered book, with red lines on the inside and letters on the outside, was handed them by a clerk, who, peering out through the bars of his office cage, said in good, strong German, "You must keep this book very carefully. Don't roll or fold it. Keep it clean and don't lose it. Be sure, now, you do not lose it. Mind what I say." What better or safer place could there be in which to hide the precious book than inside the bolster case under the pillows of the feather bed. When any errand took the old man into nearness to the bank he would often stand a moment to look the building over from roof to door-step, with a feeling of content.

The battle for bread went on and grew harder. Tins were cheaper, automobiles crowded out the horses he used to hold, German people moved away, and Italian women had no need of help with their bundles, or did not understand him. Should they begin to use the staff? Not yet; not yet. They could wait longer, until there was no work, and they were more feeble.

When the "little mother" fell and had to be carried to a hospital the old man said, "I eat so little; I will get on until she gets home, and then we must use the money." Care, kindness and skill were generously given to the "little mother,"—a foretaste of heaven; but there was the dear man alone, how her hungry heart longed for him—and the home with him was best of all.

Poor as it was, it was home, and upon her return she sought for the precious bank book. To see it again would be a joy. The big bed was opened, the gay patch-work quilt thrown back, but where was the book? It must have slipped down, or dropped behind—under the bed, perhaps. Where? The book was gone. Every corner was searched in vain. Bismarck and old Emperor William, grim and faded under cracked glass, gave no cheer as she turned the frames about to see if behind them the book could have somehow hidden itself. The old tinker joined in the search, and went out among the tins and refuse of the shop to hunt. The book was gone; surely gone!

Hoping to find it, fearing to tell of its loss, ignorant of our language, and believing that losing the book meant losing the money, the little woman kept up her search —looking, ever looking. The tinker, so sure that thieves had taken the book, felt less interest in the search, for at heart he was confident that the book had been stolen. Soon the weakness of old age crept in upon them, like an incoming tide—slowly, steadily, surely. To live they must have help. A missionary lady brought to them each month the sum which the landlord asked for the rent, a kindly nearby baker sent an occasional loaf, the market man often gave them a bag of bones and a few vegetables. So the old couple managed to keep soul and body together. But every day the "little mother" spent some of her time looking, looking.

Fresh air work, as it should be, is largely for restless, growing children; working girls are having a share in such outings to the country, to keep in health and heart for their work; old people, these grown-ups, in their second childhood, are being remembered also in fresh air plans, by generous friends who give them one day during the summer.

To such an outing, at a home near the Sound, our old couple, the tinker and his wife, were invited, with about forty others, all over sixty years of age. The journey seemed formidable; the New York Central Station seemed at the ends of the earth, and would it be safe to leave their home all day,—the lock was rickety and somebody might get in and steal. But they wanted to go,—it was a great event, this being invited to a party.

There was no question about clothes. In the hair-trunk, with its big, brass nails, relic of the old home near the Rhine, was her best gown, the one she had owned for forty years. Gowns may grow full or gowns may grow scant; they may be long or they may be short;—her one gown was to her always in fashion. When the tinker was arrayed in the old, faded blue coat and the high hat of ancient shape, decorated with many a dent, and the little wife in gown and wrap and bonnet and mitts a half-century old, they were a sight for the envy of the most burlesque of vaudeville.

Not since they went out to lay their last child in the cemetery had they been so far from home, and "little mother" timidly clung to the arm of her tall and distinguished-looking husband, never for one moment letting go her hold. The day was glorious, the sunshine and cool breeze, the great trees and broad lawns, with crested water beyond blue as the sky, made it seem like heaven to these guests from the down-town city streets.

The lunch was so delicious, served by

smiling ladies in such pretty colors, with jewels and tinkling ornaments, that the old people were silent with wonder and admiration. Never could they forget that day. Still clinging arm in arm, the old couple returned to the basement home, and after putting back into the hair-trunk their festive garments, "little mother" lighted her lamp for another search to find the missing bank book.

Some months later, as the missionary lady called with the rent, she said, "I am sorry for you, dear people, that you have not been willing to let me help you move out from this damp place. Now the law says *you must.* This building is condemned and is to be pulled down, and I am arranging for two small rooms upstairs, on the next street."

"Oh, I cannot go away! Oh, no, we must stay a little longer," pleaded "little mother," "we can't go away yet."

But the law had to take its course; they must move out.

Between the front room and the shop was—not a closet, surely; it could not rightly be called anything but a "poke-hole," hardly fit for a coal-bin. Old papers, old rags, old tins, had accumulated in it. The ever-searching German woman had spent hours with her little lamp in there until her husband had forbidden her to stay longer in the dampness. Now she begged to have everything there but the old tins, taken to the new home—nothing was she willing to throw away.

In pity, a compromise was made, and the missionary lady said, "I will bring a big light, and together we will sort over the old stuff, and then only that which can do somebody some good shall be saved; all the rest must be left for the dump-cart."

As the rags were pushed about and some of them handled, a rotten place in the old floor was seen. Boards had fallen apart and lime and broken plaster were sprinkled over the place. The quick eyes of the woman who had been for so many years looking for a leather-covered book spied something. What is it? Down into the hole she dug; there was the bank book, mouldy and stained!

"Ach, Gott, im Himmel!" she cried, tears running down her face, as she clasped it to her heart. "Mein Buch, Mein Buch!" A greedy rat had evidently tasted the corner, dragged it under the broken floor, and left it there.

Interest upon interest was added at the bank, when the missionary lady took the almost illegible book to be balanced. There was money enough to rent part of a cottage in Jersey, with a bit of land which the old man could help work, the owner of which was a young German, and his wife, whose grandparents had lived in the same village where the tinker had been a boy. There was money enough to keep the old couple in frugal comfort, "a staff to lean on" in their oldest years, and money enough to lay them away, after a little time, near their children in God's Acre.

GOING HOME

Out of the chill and the shadow
  Into the thrill and the shine;
Out of the dearth and the famine
  Into the fullness divine.
Up from the strife and the battle
  (Oft with the shameful defeat),
Up to the palm and the laurel,
  O, but the rest will be sweet!

XII

JOHN

HE home of the Wurtley family was on the top floor of a high building. Many tenements, filled to overflowing with children and adults, were below. At the last narrow stairway, the advantage of these higher rooms could be felt, for there was a rush of fresh air and a bit of real daylight. Of course there were some drawbacks. The stairs were long and the roof not quite the best, for on a rainy day, when the wind blew in a certain direction, it was necessary to put up the family umbrella over the bed. This shelter was a comfort to the tidy English mother, and a sprinkle of water mattered little to the so-called head of the house, for he was often so filled with gin

that it seemed as though a few drops of rain, if it should strike him, would only hiss and splutter like water on a hot griddle.

John Wurtley, the elder, chose this skylight home not only because the rent was cheaper, but because he disliked neighbors. His English tastes would have led him, had he been able to indulge them, to have his home shut in by a thick hedge and a high wall with a massive gateway. Even a moat with a drawbridge would have pleased him. The only one who passed by the door of their attic home was an old man who worked at night and slept all day. But practical Mrs. Wurtley saw other advantages in this abode of two rooms on the top floor, and as no one used the passageway, John, the younger, had an airy bedroom all to himself. In a corner of the hall, on a bag of excelsior and shavings, with an old comforter, the boy rested and watched the stars through his curtainless windows, the wind playing with his hair.

"No rum for me," he would mutter to himself after his father had stumbled up the stairs. "Why does mother look so white ? Rum. Why does she have to work so awful hard? Rum. Why are we hungry? Rum. No rum for me—never!" And he would pound the old ticking-bag bed with his fist.

Young John's fourteenth birthday was eventful because on that day he could go to work. He was now a man, and would "get a job." Peter, the younger brother, kept on selling newspapers before and after school. The mother's feet kept the tireless sewing machine running, for this meant bread and shelter for herself and children.

Mr. Wurtley had a good trade but earned very little more than enough to pay the saloon bill. When the fire was low and the shoes were shabby, John would grumble about Dad keeping things going all night down at the corner, where the brilliantly lighted saloon was always warm.

Mrs. Wurtley had no time or strength, no suitable clothes, and no desire to go out on the street or to make friends with anyone. With her old shawl on her head she could reach the grocery quite unnoticed, and so do any buying to which her willing boys had not attended.

Into this monotony of life a cheery, tactful missionary lady came one day in her tour of house-to-house visitation.

The tired and busy woman dropped her work for a moment and with real, natural courtesy welcomed the unknown friend. "No," she said, "I can't get out to Church, leastways, there's reasons, and as for that Mothers' Meetin'—that's not for me. I can't go, but I thank you for invitin' me. Yes, in the old country I went some times, them was better days. No, my boys don't go to no Sunday School or Meetin'—thank ye for askin', but it's all we can do to git along as we be."

Again and again the cheery lady climbed

the stairs and called on the shut-in woman. She brought to her a few flowers, or a picture card of some rural English scene, or a few papers of Sabbath Readings. The welcome was always cordial and she was always thanked for coming.

The caller did not see the father or the boys until one day when, as she climbed the stairs, a woman called out as she passed her door, "You won't git in up there,—tain't no use for you to climb any futher—them English is that proud. Her boy got in a fight and is hurt,—they're no better than none of us, if they does hold their heads up so high. You won't git in."

But the cheery lady kept on climbing, and sure enough there was young John, sitting with his swollen feet upon the edge of the washtub, while the sewing machine, as usual, was buzzing and rattling along through the long seam. The boy frowned and the mother looked anxious as the visitor entered the room, but she gave a cordial greeting and began chatting with the mother. It was as impossible to withstand the kindness of the caller as to shut out the warmth of the sunshine, and John became so interested in the story of "her boys in her Club" over at the Mission that he asked her what it would cost to join. "We fellers haven't got any places to have fun," said the boy, "nobody wants us 'cept the saloon man. He gives us a good welcome and says we needn't buy any drinks, but just come in and play cards, and when it's cold he offers us just a taste of something to warm us up. But—No, I don't—you bet—see enough of it, don't we mother?" Calls and kindness at last won John into the Club, at Sunday School he became a loyal member, and after a time he joined the Christian Endeavor Society.

Like an officer with a medal of honor John went to work one day with his C. E. badge on his coat. Poor as they were, with his stock of shirts and collars so small that it seemed impossible for him always to look the gentleman John called himself, his mother kept him neat by often taking his shirt and collar after he had gone to bed and washing and ironing them ready for the next day's use.

"Say, what you got on there," said one of the boys at the store as they ate their lunch in the basement, "C. E.—what's that?" "Come, you old dude," said another, "take it off—chuck it,—you can't play no game on us. C. E.! Take it off." At the refusal, a big bully grabbed John and put his head under the faucet. "I'll take some of your old dood starch out of you." At the next noon the battle went on; these boys filled his lunch box with sand. "That's C. E. stuff," said the bully. "Eat it or run home and tell your Ma." "You've got to take off that 'ere C. E. medal, d'ye hear?" John kept his temper so well, showed such grit in holding on to his C. E. badge, that his persecutors began to wonder, and one day the leader said,—"I say, fellers, let's go to that C. E. place and see what's it like, anyhow. We'll get up some kind of a row and have a good time,—so here's for 'C. E.' —Come on!"

They came to the Club, were welcomed and attracted, and later several joined the Sunday School group taught by the "cheery lady." Even the bully liked it all well enough to hold on for many weeks. Sunday School did not last more than two hours, Club Meeting came only once a week, and the saloon doors were always open.

The story of John's heroism in wearing the C. E. badge was related to the boys of a more fortunate class, who were pupils in a military school on the Hudson. The major and head teacher of this school had a broader outlook on the equipment for life than can be given by any curriculum of study. The pupils came from well-to-do homes, where everything that could be done for their well-being and pleasure, was looked after. But the ice-boats, the ball games, the drill, and the study, were not enough. There were Sunday night talks on how other boys live, how other boys have succeeded; and on some of these occasions John's story found an appreciative audience.

As a result, these schoolboys agreed to spend less of their spending-money allowance at the pie store, and to become responsible for the rent of a room in a downtown tenement to be called after the school, "The Mohegan Room."

The Wurtley family were moved into this tenement, and were given the use of the kitchen and one small bedroom, while Mrs. Wurtley was to use and care for the larger, "The Mohegan Room." Two of the Club boys paid for the other small bedroom. This plan was possible because Mr. Wurtley had gone away.

One big wooden rocker, a few cheap pictures, a folding bed, and a table brightened by a turkey-red cloth, well covered with magazines, papers and games which the boys of the military school sent, after they had finished with them, made an attractive home for the boys. Here came Ben and Jim and Tony and Joe, and others of their kind, and as a patron saint in the big rocker was John's mother, who sat there in the evenings mending or sewing on buttons for her boys.

When it was found best to give up the "Mohegan Room" its good work did not stop. "If you have any more young men like the John Wurtley whom you sent us," wrote the head of a large business house on Broadway, "remember there is always a place here."

As this is a true story of real people downtown a sad chapter must be added. The dark follows the light, but the sunshine always comes after the clouds. Peter did not jump quick enough with his armful of papers one night and was killed in an accident. Mr. Wurtley came back worse than ever, if that be possible, and before he died he induced his wife, the good mother of the boys, to try a little drink to drown her sorrows, and for a time she yielded to temptation.

Through all this terrible trouble John stood firm. The cheery lady was his friend, others stood by him, and when father died the death of a drunkard, mother rallied, and became again the true woman she had been through many years.

Now, at the head of a large business house in New York, John has an income which enables him to rent a very comfortable uptown apartment near a park where his wife and two children and the aged mother live happily. And, best of all, the home is a Christian home with no rum, or its associate evils.

XIII

"HIS FATHER SAW HIM"

IT was the year of hard times, and the financial wheels moved so slowly that many men willing to work could not get a job. An American family pulled up stakes in the Massachusetts town where they lived, and came to the big city, where surely there would be plenty of work.

Their savings were used carefully; but rent and food and fire and shoes made great inroads on the little fund. The big tenement house, where they lived, swarmed with men and women whose language was a jargon; and the halls were full of the smell of garlic. It was all so foreign—so different from the country town, that the little family kept very closely to themselves.

But our worker, whose district took in that part of Bleecker Street, found them, and the wife soon learned to prize her friendship, and the children watched for the coming of the silver-haired lady.

"No," said the man, to the cordial invitation, "Thank you. I ain't no use for Church or meetin's. I was a sailor a good many years, and I don't feel good under a big roof. What I want is work—work. My wife and the kids likes your mother's meetin's; they does her good, she says, and anyhow the coffee and a little visitin' seems to chirk her up—it's good of you."

A few odd jobs, here and there, were all the work the man secured. The good steady job did not turn up, and things began to look dark.

The silver watch went into pawn; then the big overcoat, the man declaring the city was so warm he did not need it. Little trinkets of early days followed, for the children were cold and hungry. At last came a sleety day, when the landlord threatened to put them all out on the street, and the wife slipped over to the place of the "three balls," and handed over her precious wedding ring.

When the husband returned, hungry and cold, and bitter at heart, and saw his wife's hand without its golden circle, he burst out into grievous words against God and man, and flinging his arms around his wife, said, "Now, I'm off; if God don't help me, the devil will—if you don't see me, I'm drowned—you'll be better off!"

With a slam of the door, and a clattering down the tenement stairs, he disappeared, and he did not come back.

What could the poor woman do but lean on the patient, loving missionary lady who had drunk of the cup of sorrow herself, and knew where to lead the distressed woman to find comfort.

Together they sought the morgue; they

From Pictorial News Co.

A WHIRLPOOL OF HUMANITY

Form every nation and clime, and from all parts of our own land, people are continually flocking into New York

visited the jail; and again took the weary trip to the morgue; police were questioned —but all in vain. The man had disappeared utterly.

Many of the lines of our work were used. House to house visitation, Mothers' Meetings, Day Nursery, had all been tried. Now we needed money to redeem the woman's warm suit and good shoes.

One institution was found where the seven-year-old boy could be cared for. We found a place where the woman could do housework, in a Jersey town, and nearby was a farmer, who would board the four-year-old girl. It was near enough to the mother so that once a week on her "day out," she could appease the hunger of her mother-heart by having her baby in her arms.

The first money she earned went to the pawn shop, and redeemed her wedding ring, and next the big shaggy great coat. "If I can't ever see him, I love to see his coat, and some day our boy maybe will wear it."

One Sunday afternoon nearly two years after this, we were at a little song service, in one of the lodging houses for men on the Bowery. At the close, the men were invited to go to the Broome Street Tabernacle for the evening meeting. A few of the men lagged along behind, and joined the crowd gathered about the steps, where a short welcoming service was carried on. The little organ was unfolded, and we began with the hymn, "Jesus is calling, Jesus is calling—Calling to-day, calling to-day." A few words followed, the theme being the Father's love for his prodigal son. In the far country the Father had not forgotten his child. He saw him even "when he was afar off." God had seen each man of this audience, in all his wanderings, and was ready with his welcome.

One man who had followed from the lodging house listened intently, with his eyes riveted, not on the speaker but on the sweet face of the missionary—our dear Mrs. Safford, gone long since to her rich reward.

At the close he quickly stood by her and touched her hand, saying, "Do you know me? Where's my wife?" A slight hesitation made the man exclaim, "For God's sake don't tell me she's dead!"

That bitter day, when the man rushed away, he found himself on the edge of the water, with the mad thought of destroying himself. A ship was just starting out; he was hailed by some one of the crew, taken aboard, and sailed away. On his return he visited his former tenement house, but only strangers with a foreign tongue answered his questions. On the Tabernacle steps, he recognized the face of the missionary lady, whom he had met in his home.

The rest of this little story is soon told. We helped bring the family together, and establish their home. The man became a

Christian. Prosperity followed. He gradually paid for a cozy house on Long Island, and he and his family are valuable members of the Church and the community.

"And he came to his father. But when he was yet a great way off, his father saw him, and had compassion, and ran, and fell on his neck, and kissed him."

XIV

SCHOLARSHIPS

LD and feeble, her home a rear tenement, Mrs. G. was yet a real Christian lady. She had been led into the joy and peace of a trust in Christ, and it shone in her wrinkled face and faded eyes.

Living with her was her dear grandchild, as sweet and bright as a bunch of heather. Well might she be called "Annie Laurie."

The grandfather had done what he could for his adopted country when he shouldered his musket and marched away behind the Stars and Stripes to do battle in the Southland: "Greater love hath no man than this—that a man lay down his life."

Because of this sacrifice, pension money came to the old widow, through the long years. It was not enough for any luxuries, but young Annie tried to help as best she could before and after school. There were errands to be done for neighbors; a baby to tend for some mother who had no caretaker for her little ones; or perhaps the windows of a tenement needed washing, and Annie on Saturday, could take off the dust and dirt and let in the sunshine. Thus, every week, Annie brought in dimes which helped the old grandmother's scanty purse. Surely "little Annie Laurie" was none the less a lady. If "a man's a man for a' that," is not a girl a lady for a' that?

In public school little Annie was at the head of her class; at Sunday School and Christian Endeavor she was a leader. As the girl matured and grew still prettier and more attractive, the need of different surroundings and more refined social life, with other opportunities for education, became very apparent. We had watched her growth, we had seen from month to month,

A BASEMENT HOME

Lighted wholly by a gas jet. The thrifty mother cleans offices and sews. Even from such a home have grown up men and women of Christian character.

and year to year the need to this young life of a different atmosphere, outside of the love and care of the old grandmother.

The gift of scholarships at the Moody Schools had been given to me by our far-sighted and generous friend, Miss Helen Gould, now Mrs. Finley J. Shepard. The question which confronted us was, would the old lady be willing to let her only companion, the child she loved and lived for, go away from her? Would she not, with her small income, realize the earning power in shop or factory of so bright a girl; and so prefer to keep her granddaughter with her? Would she realize the poor surroundings to which she had become familiar, and insist upon the really excellent advantages of the High School for which the girl was now ready?

With one of our trained nurses who had cared for the old lady at many times of sickness and had been a very special friend to little Annie, I went down to the tenement home, to put this important decision before the old grandmother, while Annie was at school. The passage way from the front of the building on the street to the rear house at the back was so narrow, that we had to hold back our skirts from the white-wash of the newly cleaned walls; carefully we passed the garbage barrels of the inner court, and entering the rear house, climbed one dark flight of stairs to Mrs. G.'s door. A smiling face greeted our coming and everything was neatness itself within; the kitchen stove shone like a mirror; the floor little Annie kept scrubbed, was as the oft quoted expression puts it, "clean enough to eat off of." The teakettle sang cheerily and cups were laid out on the table for our coming.

Sitting there together we drew the picture of the Northfield school buildings surrounded by great trees with grass and flowers, and the lovely views on every side, of the grand old hills, and the winding river. We told of the valuable instruction, the comfortable rooms, the happy girls, and the beautiful and practical training for Christian service. The old lady's face began to glow, there was no shadow nor word of her own future loneliness, and how hard it would be to live without the granddaughter, who was the life and light of her heart and home. At last she quietly said, "Wait, wait, I must see what my Lord tells me to do, I must ask Him." Mounting a wooden chair she reached up, and took down from a high shelf at the side of the room a ticking bag with something large and heavy within it. We helped her step down as she kept her bundle clasped in her arms, the ticking bag was removed, and then she came to an inner white bag and carefully brought out from it a large old family Bible in heavy binding. "You see," said Mrs. G., "the plaster is often a bit loose and shakes down on everything; I always have the outside bag to keep it off, and then a nice clean white bag is a good proper cover for my dear old Bible." With the old wrinkled hands laid on the cover there was a moment of silent prayer, and then with closed eyes the Book was opened tenderly and one old knotted finger laid on a verse in "Isaiah," which she read and then re-read, looking up at us with a smile which made the old faded, wrinkled face beautiful. The crumbling plaster, the dingy wall, the tenement houses were forgotten, all the old life slipped out of sight, and the uplift and outlook of the vision was of the kingdom of God—service for Him—and trust in His power and peace.

"Behold, I will do a new thing; now it shall spring forth; shall ye not know it? I will even make a way in the wilderness, and rivers in the desert."

"Yes," said the old lady, with the open Bible still on her lap, "my girl may go to the Christian School, the Lord tells me."

Annie went to Northfield. Not for long did the grandmother have to live alone, for God took her after a short illness from the tenement to a mansion prepared for her.

Of the honors Annie won, of the service she rendered, at school and later college, we may not write. She is not a part of our downtown life. In a distant city Annie and her educated, Christian husband are making their home an inspiration to all who come within its far reaching influence. It is a lovely and loving home such as Jesus, were He here, would, when weary at the nightfall, want to visit even as at Bethany.

Other girls and boys for whom we have worked, have made the most of their lives by means of these scholarships, so that many women and men to-day are in large places of Christian usefulness and look back gratefully to the time when they had "their chance."

A girl who determined to become a

teacher of ability had to struggle with conditions caused by the arrest of her father; yet she succeeded.

A leader of men was a boy with the awful handicap of a drunken parent.

A poor girl who desired a musical education overcame all her difficulties, and is an artist and an exceptional teacher of music to-day.

A boy whose bed consisted of two chairs or the floor, is now doing editorial work.

A lad of grit and go, whose home was very poor, is now well up in the legal profession.

An Italian lad who studied the life of Lincoln at night in his tenement room, and shined shoes on a ferryboat during the day, has now the prefix of "Honorable" to his name.

> "Honour and shame from no condition rise;
> Act well your part, there all the honour lies."

www.ingramcontent.com/pod-product-compliance
Lightning Source LLC
LaVergne TN
LVHW010604110826
845149LV00003B/769

* 9 7 8 1 4 1 8 1 8 7 4 2 2 *